debbietravis' paintedhouse

living & dining rooms

debbie travis' painted house

living & dining rooms

60 stylish projects to transform your home

Debbie Travis with Barbara Dingle

Clarkson Potter/Publishers
New York

Published by Clarkson Potter/Publishers, New York, New York.
Member of the Crown Publishing Group.

Random House, Inc. New York, Toronto, London, Sydney, Auckland
www.randomhouse.com

CLARKSON N. POTTER is a trademark and POTTER and colophon are
registered trademarks of Random House, Inc.

Printed in Japan

Design by Jan Derevjanik

Library of Congress Cataloging-in-Publication Data
Travis, Debbie.
    Debbie Travis' painted house living and dining rooms:
60 stylish projects to transform your home / by Debbie Travis
with Barbara Dingle.
        p. cm.
    1. Handicraft. 2. Interior decoration. 3. Living rooms.
4. Dining rooms. I. Title: Living and dining rooms.
II. Dingle, Barbara. III. Title.
TT157.T7235   2001
745.5—dc21   00-047895

ISBN 0-609-80550-9

10 9 8 7 6 5 4 3 2 1

First Edition

To my mother, whose favorite retreat away from me and my sisters was her living room.

acknowledgments

I would very much like to thank all those who have helped me produce this book: Margot Schupf, my editor at Clarkson Potter, for her guidance, art director Marysarah Quinn, and designer Jan Derevjanik, who made my first paperback so wonderful. My talented art director, Alison Osborne, who helped me plan living and dining rooms around each person's lifestyle and decorating dreams. Valorie Finnie and Elaine Miller, who decorated the many rooms within realistic budgets, using great style and endless patience. My incredible team of painters and artists: Stephanie Robertson, Lynn Roulston, James Simon, Sue Pistawka, Anne Coté, Allone "Mr. K" Koffkinsky, Andrejs Ritins, Durwin Rice, Melanie McSpurren, and Kristin Shannon, who designed the colorful dining room pictured on the front cover. And my right hand, Dana MacKimmie, without whom these pages would be blank. Huge thanks to George Ross who photographed the rooms so beautifully and is such a joy to work with. Thanks to Ernst Hellrung for his step-by-step photography and powers with a drill, and also to Peter Sellars.

My sincere gratitude to the homeowners who shared their decorating dilemmas with the Painted House team, and allowed us into their homes.

Hugs and kisses to Barbara Dingle, who writes with enthusiasm and dedication, and is fearless with deadlines.

Finally, and most of all, I would like to thank the loyal viewers of *The Painted House* who watch me from all over the world, and the television networks who bring the show into your living rooms.

contents

introduction

Decorating today is not just about style, it's about lifestyle—your lifestyle. It's about how you live, the people with whom you live, and the colors, textures, and patterns that you love; a look that makes you smile each time you enter the front door; and a place where your family and friends are comfortable.

Traditionally, a home was divided into a series of rooms, each with its own purpose. But the diverse needs of today's homeowners have had a profound impact on home design, altering not only the layout of the rooms but also the way we use them.

No other rooms in the house have evolved as dramatically as the living room and the dining room. Often reserved only for guests, they have always been the most underused rooms in the home, but now that role has changed. The design of modern homes has been revolutionized to capitalize on the practical use of more limited space. But many of these layout changes, such as combined living and dining areas or barrier-free open-concept plans, create major decorating challenges. If the kitchen is small, the dining area is used not just for special occasions but for every meal. Whether used for work or for celebration, the dining room is where some of our happiest memories are created. Homes with large eat-in kitchens may eliminate the need for a separate dining room, except for more formal feast days and important occasions. The space can still be used to great advantage, however, as the size of the dining table makes it an obvious choice for other tasks, such as home or office work, or spreading out a project. Domestic life has become less formal, and the living room has become exactly that—a space to live in, where the whole family gathers after a busy day to watch television, work at the computer, and play games. But it is still the room that asserts our style and the way we live, the place we use for entertaining friends.

Living and dining rooms are public rooms; they are on show to your visitors in a way that is either informal or more structured. They are the perfect places to display what you hold dear, and how you like to spend your free time. A favorite collection of dishes, frames, or wooden sculptures; the art on the wall; a handmade quilt thrown over a comfy couch; an easy chair with a perfectly poised reading lamp; or a music system with just the right speakers—all are clues to what is important to you. And because you have chosen to put these accoutrements in the open living areas of your home, your guests can share and enjoy them as well. They become a very personal and welcome gesture.

your lifestyle

We all go through many stages in our lifetime, and what may be perfectly suitable for us in our twenties when we are just starting out will soon change as we share our living space with a partner and then children. More time passes and the family structure changes again, perhaps with the addition of elderly parents to our home and the departure of grown children. Our lifestyles are in continual flux, and thus so are the ways we use our home space.

Decorating decisions for today's living and dining rooms are rooted first in our needs. Ask yourself what these rooms mean to you right now. Do you want a living room where you can relax and recharge by yourself, or a place where the whole family gathers? Is the living room furniture comfortable? Is there something interesting to look at when you sit in different areas? Is there a good reading light? Have you planned any ambient lighting? Can you view artwork easily? Are there tables nearby on which to place a drink or a snack plate?

Is the dining room reserved for parties and celebrations, or is it your everyday eating area? Dining rooms are marvelous spaces to use drama, but make sure there's enough light to see your dinner and enough padding on the seats to withstand a leisurely feast. The table is the focus of the dining room, but a rich wall finish and lighting details will help you enhance the mood.

In an open-concept design, the living and dining rooms are combined and become the central focus of the home, often used more for informal relaxing than for formal parties. The challenge is how to visually separate this large space and create a cozy, more intimate atmosphere.

How the room is going to be used will govern everything else, from the type and style of furnishings to the colors on the wall. So think about your plan and then write it down. It's your *mission statement*, and all your decorating decisions revolve around what you want that space to do.

If you are just starting out, it is a good idea to have a long-term plan for some of the decisions you will have to make. It is easy to apply a fresh coat of paint, but furnishings such as a white couch or a glass-top coffee table may not be practical when children come along, and these are expensive to replace.

There has never been a better, more exciting time to design and decorate a room. We are no longer dictated to by strict rules, a particular style, or a correct color. Today's home decorating emulates the fashion industry —anything goes! Mass media, the Internet, and knowledge of and influences from different cultures have created a global village of products, designs, and styles that are accessible and readily available to everyone. Paint manufacturers have produced lines in every possible shade and finish. Hardware stores have become design centers with easy-to-use materials and tools, all designed to help you personalize your home, and there seems to be a never-ending variety of furnishings, accessories, and fabrics.

The freedom to choose from such a broad spectrum of styles and products can create its own design dilemma. It forces you to think about what you really like instead of what's popular at the moment. But it's a wonderful feeling to create something that nourishes your spirit, which is what home is all about.

imagination, inspiration, and impact

The hardest part of beginning any decorating project is making the first move. Whether you are starting from scratch or just rearranging what you already have, the initial action can be daunting. What we all need are ideas and the confidence to put them into practice. The rooms in this book are designed around the particular lifestyle of each homeowner. As you can see from the "before" pictures, their challenges were numerous, both typical and varied. Happily, we were able to meet these criteria, working within the architecture and proportions of the rooms, with the existing furniture, and in keeping with the way they live.

There are three elements to consider when you first begin to plan a room: imagination, inspiration, and impact. Be free with your imagination; let it soar, even if everything you envision is unrealistic to put into practice. Be inspired by the world around you. A holiday taken in Mexico can motivate you to use a variety of textures; a Mediterranean cookbook can tantalize your taste buds for color; nature is full of colors, patterns, and textures; and there are endless decorating books and magazines filled with style ideas and numerous ways of placing furnishings. When you go out to restaurants and hotels, look for design details.

mixing styles

We have developed four basic room types in this book: contemporary, traditional, themed, and country. Perhaps you are not sure which style suits you or are confused because you're fond of a modern glass-and-wrought-iron dining table but also love Granny's old rocker. You can take ideas from all four groups and mix and adapt them to suit your own lifestyle and personal taste.

You can live in a contemporary home deep in the countryside or successfully create a country home inside a city apartment. Many of us desire a Zen-like space that soothes the soul, but this may not be possible for a family with small children, whose main priorities are comfort and joy. Tradition is often an important factor. We like to surround ourselves with our memories and inherited pieces but would also like to add elements of drama or fantasy for evenings of entertainment.

Mix styles to suit yourself. If you like an unorthodox combination of new and old, chances are it will look terrific.

the main ingredients

If you are not sure where to start, there are three ingredients that help to create a perfect ambience in a room: color, texture, and pattern. They are the most important considerations for any interior design scheme, no matter where they are applied: walls, floors, ceiling, furniture and accessories, or window treatments. All play a part in making your room fit together as a harmonious whole. Experiment by mixing color, texture, and pattern, and you will create decorating solutions for your living and dining rooms that sing.

color

Color is a powerful tool and is intensely personal. It affects our emotions in many ways. Color can relax us, stimulate conversation, and make us feel happy or sad. We all react to it differently. What is cheerful and fun to one person may appear too bright and garish to another. Lavender living room walls with lime green trim are remarkably refreshing and youthful, but they're not for everybody. A shade of yellow may be delicate and subtle in a living room but harsh and difficult to live with in a bedroom.

We all have prejudices and reject certain colors for interior design. You may think you could never live in a brown room, but the new sultry shades of chocolate, peat, and frothy cream are contemporary and chic. The look of a particular color will vary depending on where it is used. Tastes do change over the years, so keep an open mind: You may be surprised and delighted with a whole new color palette that you never thought you could live with.

creating a color scheme

The selection of paint colors is unlimited, and today manufacturers have made it easier to pick a color scheme by grouping colors into workable shades, themes, moods, and even by historic periods, such as the Heritage palette, or by decades like the '60s. This dazzling array of choices can be intimidating, so a degree of confidence is required. Instead of opting for beige again, realize that if you do make a mistake with your color choice, your walls can be repainted.

If you plan to repaint your living or dining room, begin by assessing which furnishings will stay in the room and pick out one color from among them that appeals to you. Start to build a palette by adding colors and shades that work together and create the mood you are looking for. How the room will be used, who will use it, and when (in the daytime or evening) all dictate the color scheme. Choose no more than three paint colors to avoid making the room look too busy. The dominant color will go on the walls and the others on the woodwork and trim. Accent colors can be added in the form of cushions or window treatments, or even through a painting or a photograph.

I always recommend that you buy the smallest containers sold of the colors you've chosen and apply test patches to each area. Live with these swatches for a few days and place furniture in front of them; when you're happy that the scheme works, buy the remainder of the paint.

When you are planning *where* to paint each color, the simplest guideline is to apply the lighter colors at the top of the room. A relatively neutral palette may include a white ceiling, off-white crown moldings, pale ocher walls above a dado, and terra-cotta below. The whole room can be framed with white baseboards and trim.

There are many color theories, lists of dos and don'ts, the infamous color wheel, and, of course, tons of advice from the experts (myself included), but when it's all said and done, a successful color scheme is what makes *you* feel positive and happy.

texture

There is a visual and tactile allure to a textured surface that is common to all cultures. The Victorians loved thick velvets and brocades, and ornately carved architectural details. In the 1970s, shag carpets and grass-cloth walls were popular. Mediterraneans love the rough and weathered textures of stone. Asian sensibilities revere satin gloss furniture finishes and natural fiber matting. Textural contrasts are very satisfying to look at and live with. It's the juxtaposition of smooth materials against rough, thick fibers next to thin, raised plaster over a flat wall that pleases us.

The use of texture as a decorating tool has become more interesting today. Urban homes play with tradition by using rugged barn woods in clean modern settings. Embossed wallpapers are popular once again, and plaster finishes have been reinvented with a variety of textured surfaces. Textured natural elements, such as bamboo, grasses, cane, and sisal, are adorning walls, furniture, and floors. The smoothness of glass against the warmth of wood creates incredible contrasts that work beautifully in modern homes.

Water-based paints and glazing liquids have revolutionized the ability to apply affordable faux textured finishes to walls. The translucent nature of a colored glaze allows you to create depth simply by applying it over an opaque base coat. By using these glazes and a few simple tools, it is possible to imitate the look of fabrics such as silk and suede, building materials like wood, marbles, and stonework, and precious metals.

A combination of textures promotes an aura of luxury simply because it feels good. Walk barefoot across a varnished hardwood floor, then sink into scrunchy shag carpet; caress the weave of a smooth cotton upholstery fabric or the nubbly strands of a woolen cushion fringe. Today's natural and synthetic materials are blending together so that it is no longer a costly matter to surround yourself with the feeling of luxury.

pattern

Traditionally, a vast array of different patterns was used to decorate the home. Floral and flocked wall coverings, chintz and paisley fabrics for upholstery and window coverings, and Persian carpets and multicolored floor tiles were chosen to combat somber Victorian homes with their dark wood paneling, high ceilings, and mazelike floor plans. Modern architecture has opened up home design, and the use of patterns has become simplified. Pattern is seen today in a more subtle light, through sheers draped softly over a huge window or a series of neutral stripes painted horizontally across a wall. Instead of a ruling form, pattern has become an accent or focal point, bordering a fireplace or an interesting architectural detail.

Pattern can be the drama or the personality of a decorated room. Use it in all its forms to break up a large area of solid color or to distinguish one room from another in an open-concept plan. A favorite pattern found in a piece of fabric or in a magazine can be duplicated on fabric, wood, walls, floors, and virtually any surface with paint. Choose colors that come from or complement the pattern, repeat sections of it in other areas of the room, or use it to tie two or more rooms together.

If you study nature, you'll notice how the sun and clouds create shadows, how layers of branches and rock face are mirrored in a lake, or how trees form a parade line along a roadway. These beautiful images can be transferred to your rooms in the form of patterns on fabric or the setup of furnishings. Sun through a slatted window blind will cast shadows that change throughout the day. A lineup of dining chairs, the configuration of artwork on the walls, even the planks of a wood floor all add layers of pattern and interest to your space.

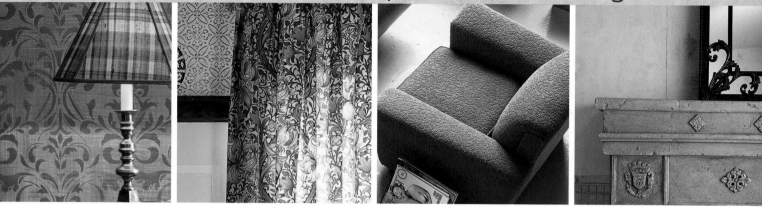

Decorating a room successfully takes some thought about all the elements that make up the whole effect. To establish a pleasing environment, the colors, lighting, window treatments, and furnishings all work together harmoniously; as in a good marriage, they help bring out the best in one another. Consider each of these elements separately, and discover how much they can do for your living and dining rooms.

lighting

We usually think about how we are going to light a room at the end of the design process, once all the other elements are in place, but good lighting is essential to any decorating scheme. It is far better to approach the subject when you first decide on the color scheme, furnishings, and fixtures for the room. The wrong lighting can make a fabulous wall color or even a favorite piece of furniture seem lifeless. Just like a haphazard color scheme, bad lighting can make us feel tired or overly stressed; poor lighting can also cause accidents. Whereas a badly lit room can be unforgiving to you and your decor, good lighting will enhance a color scheme and bring your furnishings and fabrics to life.

Clever lighting can also be used as a decorating solution for the not-so-perfect room by camouflaging an unattractive area. Several up-lights that bathe the walls in light can make small rooms look more spacious. Large rooms that feel too formal can be brought down to a cozier scale with a few table lamps scattered throughout the area.

The living room requires the most varied lighting because it's a multi-purpose space used not only for watching television and reading but also for entertaining. You may have bookshelves, paintings, or favorite objects that deserve highlighting. The dining room is designed around two purposes—eating and entertaining—and all the action takes place in one area, around the table. The lighting here is an important key not only to creating the right mood but to ensuring that your guests and your table look their best. A dimmer switch is a good idea to control the light both when you are preparing the room and later when the guests are seated and candles lit.

You should consider six types of lighting when designing a living or dining room: natural, ambient, accent, task, decorative, and kinetic. Effective lighting does not necessarily reflect a large budget, but a good imagination and some thought are essential.

natural lighting

When you pick a color scheme, it's important to consider the amount and intensity of sunlight that a room receives. Paint colors change, often dramatically, not only room by room but also on each wall, depending on the source of light. Natural light is always welcome; it makes colors more true, and it's easiest on the eyes when reading or working. If sunlight streams into your room at any time of day, why not embrace this element by using shutters or translucent sheers to diffuse the light, creating an intriguing daytime mood.

ambient lighting

This type of lighting has a psychological effect on the mood of a room. Although natural daylight is also ambient lighting, we really think of the effect this emcompassing light creates after dark. It can come from several sources and should be bright, but not garish. You can use a combination of wall sconces that direct the light up to the ceiling, an overhead light that shines downward to the floor, and lamps that create pools of light to wash a room with soft light. The ambience can be controlled by using all or some of the lights and dimmers to strike the appropriate mood.

accent lighting

Once the ambient lighting is in place, you should consider accent lighting. This is a way to highlight favorite objects, pic-

tures, or interesting architectural details. Spotlights in the ceiling, tiny shelf lights in a curio or china cabinet, and photo lights are all designed for this purpose. Plants usually respond better to up-lighting. Although the main purpose of accent lighting is to favor the interesting parts of a room, it is also a great trick for drawing attention away from pieces of furniture that are useful but not attractive, such as a television or a plain bookcase, or even a dull corner. Accent lighting produces shadows and reflections that build on a room's atmosphere and mood.

task lighting

This is the type of lighting required for particular tasks, such as reading, writing, or sewing in the living room or serving in the dining room. The light should shine directly over the work area and should be bright enough so that you can see comfortably without squinting or straining your eyes. The best task lights have reflectors that cast light in a particular direction and can be adjusted by height and angle as well as strength.

decorative lighting

You may fall in love with a chandelier for your dining room that gives very little useful light, but the piece is fabulous and fits your decor perfectly. This is decorative lighting. Task and ambient lighting come from other sources. A fascinating floor lamp or unusual ceiling fixture can become the focal point of your room. Candlelight is also mainly decorative. Interesting candles come in every shape, size, and scent, and their holders are just as imaginative. The decoration on a dining room table can revolve around a collection of romantic candles.

kinetic lighting

Kinetic lighting is purely for fun. It is about movement rather than serving a function. The dancing flames of a roaring fire or flickering candlelight is kinetic light in its simplest form. The current popularity of the '50s Retro style has seen the resurgence of Lava lamps and revolving lights. Flickering bulbs provide very little useful light but can be used to replicate flames and candlelight.

window treatments

Nothing dates a room quite like the window treatment. If you look through decorating books and magazines from the 1980s, you'll see busy, balloon curtains with swags and drapes that appear very out of style today. Contemporary designers focus more on the architecture of the window itself. Windows can be your room's biggest asset. They let in light in all its variety and bring the outside into the home. Traditional draperies will always have a place in living and dining rooms designed around specific periods, such as the Victorian or Georgian eras. For more modern spaces, especially lofts and homes with oversized windows, it is popular and certainly more economical to casually hang yards of simple, lightweight fabric from hoops or clamps to blur rather than block out exterior views.

blinds and shutters

Once bare and rather cold, blinds have evolved into one of the most popular decorative window treatments. Venetian blinds are available in a variety of natural woods, or painted or stained any color. Metal, mesh, even bamboo venetian blinds will allow the light to filter into a room during the day and give privacy at night. Roman blinds that fit neatly inside window frames can be customized with coordinating fabrics and lined with blackout fabric to completely block out the light.

Used for centuries in hot Mediterranean countries to keep out the scorching sun, shutters are a great alternative to blinds and are extremely stylish. They can be custom-cut or bought ready-made in hardware stores. Salvage yards always have an interesting selection of old shutters that can be cut to size and refinished to suit your style.

ready-made curtains

It has never been easier to hang curtains than it is today. Available in plain and patterned sheers, cottons, and linens, ready-made curtains are cut to fit most standard windows. Complex and costly drapery hardware has been replaced by simple wooden or wrought-iron hanging rods enhanced by every style of finial. Some curtains come with tabs or loops at the top that you just need to thread over a rod. Fabric panels can also be attached to rods or even wire with rings and clips.

making your own curtains

If ready-made curtains do not fit your decor or the size of your windows, then you can easily make your own—and you do not need to be a seamstress. There is a huge selection of inexpensive fabric to choose from. In this book, we use Indian sari fabrics for their lush sheers on page 115 and lengths of felt to create the look of a more luxurious cashmere on page 53. Never skimp on the amount of fabric used—the curtains should pool slightly onto the floor and be at least one and a half times wider than the window. Use your imagination when attaching the curtains to the rods. I fold leather drawer pulls into rings on page 53, or you can make your own finials from a variety of different materials (see page 115). The oversized industrial windows of loft apartments can often be difficult and costly to treat, but they do require some form of privacy. Panels of sheer fabric attached tautly to metal swing arms at the top and bottom of the window are a contemporary solution.

traditional window treatments

There will always be room for fabulous rich curtains in a traditional setting, though they are often very expensive because of the amount of fabric and tailoring required. There are several tips to reduce the cost: Velvets always create a sumptuous look, and they are available in less expensive, lighter weights. The trick is to add a thick inner lining to make the velvet feel and look heavier than it really is. A gorgeous piece of fabric or light tapestry can be swagged over a wooden or wrought-iron rod capped with stunning finials to produce a luxurious treatment without having to buy many yards. Valances can be cut from medium-density fiberboard (MDF) and decorated with paint for detail (see page 82). Blinds and curtains can be combined for an inexpensive but dramatic effect.

furnishings

Furniture is not only functional—it contributes a major statement to the style of your room. Few of us begin from scratch when we furnish a room. We all have pieces that we love, but we also may need furniture that does not fit our style. Since budget is often a consideration, we have to work with what we have. This is where imagination and invention come into play. You can transform tables with paint or completely reinvent them with a new top (see page 129), and recover sofas and dining chairs.

When you are starting out, plan a room that can evolve and grow, not one that's finished all at once. Try to have one good item in your living or dining room. It may be a treasured antique, a fabulous mirror, or a set of beautiful cushions. This piece will automatically draw the eye and it can also be your starting point for the design of the room. Remove furnishings that you no longer like or that have no useful function. Give them to some-one else, have a yard sale, or move them to another room where they will be put to better use. If you simplify your rooms by removing unwanted clut-ter, you and your guests will enjoy what you have and feel more comfortable.

sofas and chairs

A fabulous sofa can be the focal point of a living room. This is a big invest-ment, so it is wise to think about the future before buying. White silk may not be the way to go if you plan to have children or own a rambunctious dog. To start, choose a neutral color in a hard-wearing fabric: A sofa with a great shape can always be reupholstered in a more exciting style once the children are grown. Sofas and chairs are being designed in a fascinating variety of materials. Traditional pieces are covered in rich tapestries and tactile chenilles. The natural look of reed and wicker has been given a slightly more formal air for use indoors. For contemporary settings there are brushed metal frames and even molded plastic.

If you don't like what you have, but can't afford to replace it just yet, there are solutions. Reupholstering a sofa can sometimes cost as much as a

new one, and it is only worth the expense if you love the shape and style of the piece. Strong cotton or canvas slipcovers are practical and less expensive; they are the best way to camouflage worn or dated materials. Avoid slipcovering leather sofas, since the covers will always move and slide. If your budget is really tight, then the best solution is a throw rug and a few bright and cheerful cushions.

secondhand classics

A can of paint and some sandpaper can transform just about any type of old furniture to fit the style of a room. Yard sale finds and inherited pieces, even old doors and moldings, can be used in an inventive way to dress a space. When you are searching for secondhand furniture, look at the shape rather than the finish. If the shape is interesting, imagine what it would look like with a new color, a paint finish, or new hardware. If a piece is damaged, consider carefully whether it can be fixed and at what cost before purchasing.

For modern rooms, hunt down mid-twentieth-century furnishings with steel and aluminum frames, or select clean-lined shapes from the '50s and '60s and repaint them in high-energy colors. For traditional homes, look for old leather chairs, although it's getting hard to find them. Coffee tables are new to the twentieth century and seem to be limited in choice. You can make your own coffee table by cutting down the legs of a full-size table to create an oversized piece. Tray tables from the '40s are easy to find, and can be reinvented with decoupage or a new stain and coats of varnish.

buying new furniture

Shopping for furniture is often a daunting and frustrating business. Mistakes can be costly, so take your time and remember that most good furniture stores will let you try a piece at home before you buy. What looks fabulous on the showroom floor can be completely out of place in your living or dining room. Always go shopping armed with room measurements, color swatches, and even pictures of your room. If you see a style that inspires you in a magazine, take that too.

If you decide to buy new, choose pieces that you feel you can live with for many years and adapt to changes in the colors and style of your room. Buy the best furniture that you can afford, whether pieces from today's innovative designers or antiques that will never lose their value.

fireplaces

Even though the need for a fireplace has changed dramatically over the last fifty years, it is still one of the most sought-after features when buying a home. A fireplace is a natural focal point; it draws the eye and creates a warmth and sense of home even in the most contemporary settings.

reinventing a dated fireplace

An ugly brick fireplace can overshadow even the most fabulous decor. Restored brick chimney breasts in Victorian homes are quite beautiful, but the cheaper brick used later in the twentieth century looks very ordinary. You can paint brick, but you cannot disguise its shape. The best way to reinvent a brick fireplace is to plaster the surface with a textured or smooth finish and repaint it (see page 75). The existing mantel can be changed to alter the proportions.

fake fireplaces

A fireplace does not have to work to be a design element. You can buy ready-made mantels and install them against a main wall and dress up the fire hole with a beautiful ornament, such as a basket of dried flowers or a wrought-iron grate filled with logs. A surround and mantel can be built from stock molding and MDF (see Georgian Living Room, page 64). For a unique and enticing contemporary approach, combine a dual-purpose shelving unit with flicker bulbs installed just for effect (see page 31).

It's time for you to begin decorating. Make a list, write down your mission statement, be aware of what pleases you, and look through the living and dining rooms in this book for ideas and inspiration. It's not possible, nor is it necessary, to complete an entire redecorating project in one weekend. Enjoy making one change at a time. If you follow the easy step-by-step instructions we've provided, you can transform your living areas to suit yourself and wow your guests.

contemporary
rooms

Whether you live in a tiny apartment, a suburban home, or a city loft, in contemporary rooms the accent is on clean, uncluttered surfaces and colors that are soothing but also inviting. These rooms are often meditative spaces to which we retreat from a busy day. Interest is introduced quietly through the subtle play of geometric shapes: straight lines, stripes, simple or bold blocks of color, and texture adding dimension to the color scheme. Water has always been an important decorating tool for tranquil living, and its essence can be captured in the building materials you use, such as a liquid, translucent floor surface, glass tabletops, and indoor fountains. In a contemporary room the traditional three-piece furniture suite is often replaced by mixed pieces, from a pair of modern chairs that offer a splash of color to earthbound furnishings such as reed, wicker, and brushed metal made comfortable with cotton or canvas pillows and seat covers. Windows simply dressed with translucent sheers or textured fabric become an important feature; heavy draperies give way to shutters and wooden blinds. These lighter window treatments, still provide a degree of privacy but allow the light to dance across the room as well. Contemporary style loves to play with materials in innovative ways, bringing industrial products into the home. Plexiglas panels surround a fireplace; metal finishes accent furnishings and walls. Paint finishes are understated but dazzling in their simplicity. Off-whites, creams, and pastels are grouped together for just a hint of contrast. A bold accent of color adds a modern touch, from blocks of color on a concrete floor to a bright cherry red vase.

Artists were the first to see the benefits of loft living. They loved these open-concept plan studios that afforded great light to work by and ample space for hanging canvases or creating sculptures. Over the last thirty years, many urban factories and warehouses have been converted into living spaces, and now the type of lofts available are as varied as the people who wish to live in them. Although some buildings are renovated to a high standard, many come with their original features; concrete floors, brick walls, huge windows, and exposed plumbing. Decorating such an open and stripped-down space is challenging; the ceiling and window height alone is something we're not accustomed to, and it may be difficult to envision setting up house in an area that lacks the traditional structure of separate rooms. But these are precisely the elements that make lofts so appealing.

"I call this loft my enchanted place. I always loved it,

but I wanted it to feel a little warmer, a little homier."

When I first saw this loft, where twenty-seven-year-old Chantal lives, it was just the bare bones of an old knitting factory. Because it was a rental, she did not want to go to the expense of applying drywall or boxing in the pipes, so our challenge was to use the original features to create a modern and peaceful sanctuary. Her bedroom is on the mezzanine and looks down onto the living area and the old concrete floor. I decided to make this floor the focal point, to draw the eye away from the bare industrial elements on the ceiling and walls. A palette of spicy colors divides up the space into the living areas of hall, home office, and living and dining areas. I left the walls white except for an area under the stairs, which became her home office.

Fireplaces are rare in lofts, but I added the next best thing by building a shelving unit from MDF and incorporating a simple lighting unit into it. A single layer of beach pebbles contributes another textural dimension. The inviting glow from the lights, along with the cinnamon, curry, and nutmeg tones on the floor, are modern and hip, but their warmth helped transform an industrial space into a home.

before

This loft is a large space with huge windows, exposed pipes across the ceiling, and a mix of concrete block and brick walls. The original concrete floor was in poor condition, but the eclectic mix of furnishings suited the inhabitant's needs perfectly.

loft living

The area under the stairs makes an ideal space for a home office. The floor has been blocked off in taupe and the wall painted cinnamon. This is the only wall area in the loft that has color. To highlight the cheap pine staircase, we added a trim of white paint down the edge of the steps and risers, creating a zigzag effect. Pine four-by-fours hold up the mezzanine and have been wrapped with aluminum dryer exhaust tubing to add to the industrial feel of the loft.

painted concrete floor

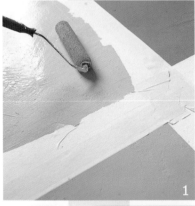

Because this loft was originally a knitting factory, there were holes in the floor where the machines had been attached. We repaired these with concrete filler and left it to dry and cure. (Depending on the depth of the hole and the humidity this can take from 4 to 7 days.) The floor was then thoroughly washed and dried. Two coats of white exterior deck and porch paint were applied to the concrete. This white base coat became the dividing border between the colors. Once the floor was thoroughly dry, 3 coats of high-sheen varnish were applied. Glossy floors will always add a modern touch to a contemporary room.

To paint the floor, **(Shot 1)** we taped off a large grid, dividing up the area into separate living spaces as walls would—hall, home office, living room, dining room. Using a roller with a long handle, we filled in the squares with different colors of latex paint. **(Shot 2)** We removed the tape and left the paint to cure for several days, then applied 3 coats of high-gloss acrylic varnish.

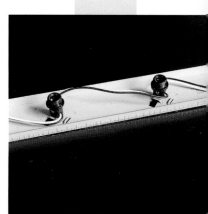

We built a shelving system from planks of MDF and painted it matte black. A length of makeup mirror lights was installed and candle-flame bulbs were used to re-create the dancing flames in a real fireplace. These bulbs can be changed to fit any mood or occasion. As a finishing touch, a single layer of beach pebbles was strewn across the base. These pebbles can be bought at garden centers by the bag. The contrasts between the rough texture of the stones against the smooth matte black shelves, the flat white walls, and the high-gloss floor are the keys to an interesting contemporary style.

White is a reflective color that enhances every color that surrounds it. Flat white latex paint can be the most uninspiring wall finish, but if you mix it with very small quantities of color, you can create a variety of off-whites that can be as enriching as any dark color. White is at its most fascinating when it is entwined with texture—imagine fluffy white towels or a bleached pine floor, roughly painted white plaster or a high-gloss white floor that reflects like glass. It's no wonder that white is a favorite backdrop for homes: Easy to choose and tint, white works with so many textures and other colors.

"This room was conceived for a young urbanite who chooses to live in a clean, uncluttered space surrounded by cool, sleek surfaces."

This room is contemporary and minimal, but each surface is special and carries its own intriguing depth. It's calm, it's cool, and the entire decor is built up around shades of white, each with a different sheen. The white walls are broken up subtly with a deceptively simple technique called shadow striping. Instead of using two different shades of paint, stripes of high-gloss varnish are applied. The contrast between the sheens of the paint and varnish produces this soft effect, which changes dramatically in day and night lighting. The floor looks positively liquid. To create this look, white paint tinted with a touch of green was applied over Russian birch plywood (which is smoother than the regular-grade plywood most commonly used on subfloors). The top coat is the one that gives the remarkable finish—a translucent epoxy varnish that goes on like a gel. One coat is the equivalent of fifty coats of standard varnish, and the finish is liquid smooth.

One of the biggest comebacks in contemporary furnishings is Plexiglas. We applied it in panels to the fireplace, using industrial bolts to secure it to the flat surround that was painted the same sea foam green as the floor. The ordinary door was given punch by building a 3-D effect with an easy trompe l'oeil design using four pastel shades.

To balance the smooth glasslike surfaces on the floor and fireplace, we decorated the room with a range of tactile furnishings: sea grass chairs, a bamboo table, and a shag rug. The effect is young, modern, and hip.

I was asked to design a set of four living spaces for a home show, each with a different philosophy. The model rooms had plain white walls, hollow-core doors with inset panels, standard moldings and trim, and a box-style fireplace, a style similar to that of a typical living room in a new home today. The other model rooms are on pages 54, 84, and 106.

hot white

shadow stripes

MATERIALS AND TOOLS

off-white latex paint, satin

roller and paint tray

pencil and ruler

chalk line

level

low-tack painter's tape

high-gloss acrylic varnish

burnt umber pure pigment (optional)

3" foam brush

Vertical stripes are the simplest form of a repeat pattern and visually raise the ceiling as the eye is drawn upward. They can be any width, and you can create them in a variety of ways. A strong color contrast will produce a pronounced and dramatic effect, but I wanted a quieter mood, so I chose an off-white base coat with a satin sheen and applied the stripes using varnish with a high-gloss sheen. I added a touch of burnt umber to tint the varnish, but it is the contrast between the sheens that creates this delicate striped effect.

Prepare your surface following the instructions in the preparation chapter, pages 162–63.

step 1   Apply 2 coats of off-white base coat and let dry for 4 hours.

step 2   **(Shot 1)** Measure and mark off the stripes; use a chalkline and the level to create straight lines. Our stripes are irregular, measuring 10"–16" wide. Mask off the stripes with low-tack tape.

step 3   If you want to add a little color to the varnish, stir ⅛ teaspoon of pigment into 1 quart of varnish. Mix well. Apply 1 coat of varnish to every alternate stripe with the foam brush. If the stripes are not dark enough, add a second coat of tinted varnish. Remove the tape carefully and let dry.

Water and glass play a big role in decoration today. This floor treatment encompasses both by combining a pale sea foam base with a translucent epoxy top coat. The durable finish appears to float.

MATERIALS AND TOOLS

water green (sea foam) latex paint, satin
roller with extension pole and paint tray
a 2-component epoxy
mixing container
large spatula
or
high-gloss acrylic varnish and foam
*   roller (if you don't use the epoxy)*

Prepare your surface following the instructions in the preparation chapter, pages 162–63.

step 1 Prime the floor and let dry for 4 hours.

step 2 Apply 1 coat of pale green base coat. Let dry for 4 hours and then apply a second coat. Let dry overnight.

step 3 **(Shots 1 and 2)** Mix the epoxy according to the directions on the package. Pour the epoxy onto the floor in workable patches, and spread it out with the spatula. Continue to pour and spread out the gel-like epoxy until the surface of the floor is covered. It is self-leveling, so don't worry about getting it perfectly even. You do need to work quickly, though, as it begins to dry in about 5 minutes. (If you are using acrylic varnish rather than epoxy, apply at least 5 coats over the paint with a foam roller to build a thick but translucent glossy layer, sanding lightly between coats.)

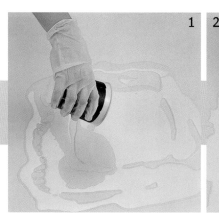
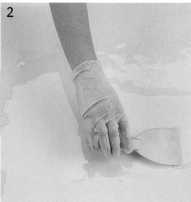

trompe l'oeil door panels

The paint technique creates a 3-D effect for the panels in this door, adding color, depth, and interest. If your door is flat, first measure and mask off the panels, then follow these instructions for the same look. The idea is to create shadow and accent panel stripes. Find your light source; the lighter accent shade runs down the side furthest from the light source and the dark shadow runs down the closer side. In this photo, our light source was coming from the left, hence the pale colors are top and right and the darker colors are bottom and left.

MATERIALS AND TOOLS

white latex paint, semigloss

3" paintbrush or small roller and paint tray

low-tack painter's tape

pale pink, medium gray, light gray, and pale turquoise latex paint, semigloss

1" paintbrush or artist's brush

Prepare your surface following the instructions in the preparation chapter, pages 162–63.

step 1 Apply 2 coats of white base coat and let dry for 4 hours or overnight.

step 2 **(Shot 1)** Mask off a triangle at the bottom of each panel with low-tack tape. Using the artist's brush, fill in these triangles with medium gray paint.

step 3 **(Shot 2)** Mask off a triangle at the top of each panel. Fill in these triangles with pale pink paint. Let all the triangles dry for 4 hours, then remove the tape.

step 4 **(Shot 3)** Tape along the right side of each panel's center line, ending at the triangles. Also tape along the inside edge of the painted triangles so that you will have a clean edge where the paint colors meet. Fill in the left side with light gray paint. Remove the tape. Let dry for 4 hours.

step 5 **(Shot 4)** Tape along the left side of each panel's center line and inside the triangles where the paint colors meet. Fill in the right side with pale turquoise paint. Remove tape, then let dry for 4 hours.

fireplace

The unique glass facade for this fireplace complements the cool tempo of the living room. To replicate the color of glass, I painted the surround the same pale green as the floor. After a grid for the panels was measured and marked off, the Plexiglas panels, which were cut to measure at the hardware store, were attached to the surround with washers and screws.

Pietro Fornasetti was known as a "Designer of Dreams," a visionary whose work has inspired many architects and furniture and fashion designers. He lived and worked in Milan, Italy, from 1935 until his death in 1988. Fornasetti's style was based on illusion. His most famous image is that of a woman devoid of expression, and he turned out over 500 versions of this enigmatic face, most of them on dinner plates. His designs are once again hugely popular in contemporary settings, and we can see his signature on china, light fixtures, furniture, and clothing. It was Fornasetti's great talent for turning everyday things into unique, whimsical objects that was the inspiration behind this dining room. The images on these pages are protected by the Fornasetti copyright.

"Although our dining room had wonderful high ceilings and was a good size, we longed to restyle the space into a room that would be a dramatic conversation piece."

When Martin and Patrice moved into a Victorian-style home, their mission was to reinvent the dining room. Sage green walls and country pine furniture no longer appealed to their sense of style. The dilemma was how to transform a country look to a modern one without spending a fortune. After I showed them the designs of the great Italian designer Pietro Fornasetti, the men were hooked. Drama was of key importance, and we began with the bold and exotic contrast of aubergine and chartreuse paint for the walls and ceiling. The white moldings that divide these two colors were then given more distinction with a strip of black-and-white images of Roman architecture. I kept the original pine table, but cut a larger, circular top. The old base and new top were painted jet black and decoupaged with Fornasetti's most well known image—a woman's face. Funky but comfortable office chairs replaced the country pine seating, and I used simple modern bookshelves as display cabinets, turned one on its side, attached legs and created a unique console table. I embellished an oversized mirror with a stunning frame of silver leaf laid over chartreuse paint. The mirror sits on the floor reflecting the ambiance of the new room.

before

This is a beautiful room in a Victorian house, but the country colors and furnishings no longer suited the home-owners' taste.

fornasetti
dining room

We reinvented the small country pine table into a slick, modern piece of furniture that now seats eight comfortably. We cut a circle from medium density fiberboard (MDF) and attached it to the original base. The entire surface was primed and then painted with two coats of semigloss black latex. The sheen is unimportant at this stage as the overall piece will be varnished as the final touch, but matte black is hard to work with as every finger mark shows. A black-and-white photocopy of a Fornasetti design was decoupaged on the center of the table with wallpaper glue; any favorite image would suffice. Masking tape was used to block out sun rays of white paint, and once dry, I used a silver indelible marker and ruler to outline the edge of each ray. Six coats of water-based gloss varnish were applied for sheen and to seal in the decoupage.

architectural border

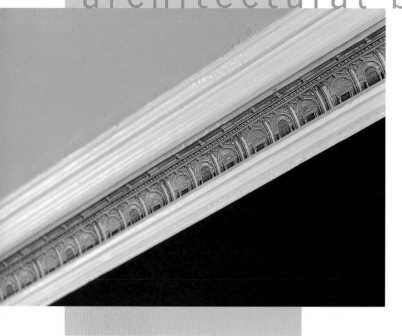

Photocopies of Roman buildings were copied to the same size, overlapped lightly and glued together to create strips of pattern, like a wallpaper border. Each length was then glued with wallpaper paste and pressed into the curve of the ceiling molding. The architectural detail makes an interesting division between the bright chartreuse ceiling and the rich aubergine walls.

contemporary console

An inexpensive shelving unit was restyled into a contemporary console by attaching legs (bought individually) to one side. The shelves now sit horizontally rather than vertically.

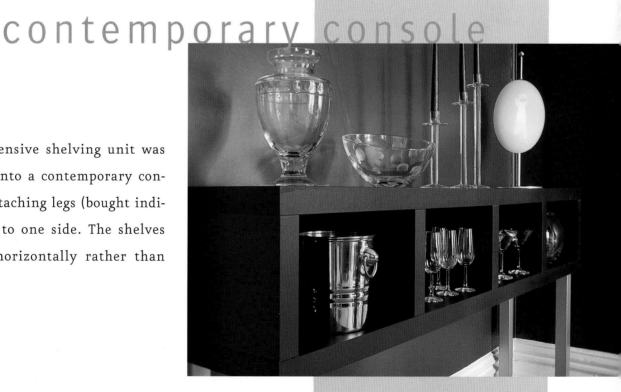

fornasetti light

Fornasetti furniture, accessories and light fixtures can be found in fine decorating stores. See Resources, page 172.

oversized mirror

Today's oversized furniture is incredibly chic when used in the right place. To open up the dining room, we made this huge framed mirror to sit propped up against the wall. A piece of MDF was cut the size of the mirror plus 5″ all around for a border. Then 5″ wide strips of MDF were glued down along the border to build the mirror frame. We applied silver leaf to decorate the frame. Traditionally, the base coat for silver leaf is black, but we used the brighter chartreuse from the ceiling for a younger, more contemporary look. It is important to apply a couple of coats of varnish to seal and protect the leaf.

MATERIALS AND TOOLS

Frame made of MDF or wood

chartreuse latex, satin

2″ paintbrush

dry adhesive transfers (see resources, page 172)

flat plastic or wooden stick

silver or aluminum leaf (aluminum is cheaper and just as nice)

soft brush

spray varnish

step 1 Prime and apply two coats of the chartreuse base coat to the frame. Let dry for 4 hours.

step 2 Cut long strips of dry adhesive to fit the surface and sides of the frame.

step 3 **(Shot 1)** Place the dry adhesive sticky side down on the frame and rub the sheet with the wood or plastic stick. (Metal will rip the paper.) Make certain that all the dry adhesive is transferred to the frame as the silver leaf will not adhere to spots where adhesive is missing. Remove the transfer paper.

step 4 **(Shot 2)** Carefully place the silver leaf onto the frame and smooth it out gently with a soft brush.

step 5 Apply 3 coats of spray varnish. Always wear a mask and work in a well-ventilated area when spraying.

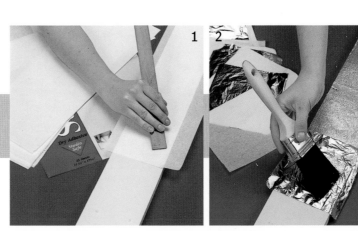

Architecture in the 1960s featured buildings devoid of all decorative detail. Modular was the flavor of the day, and boxlike rooms were stacked one on top of the other. Over the last thirty years construction in suburban neighborhoods has boomed. The details of quality construction have been replaced by homes knocked together as quickly as possible using the minimum amount of labor. Sadly, the workmanship of master craftsmen—the stonemason, the bricklayer, the skilled carpenter, the artisan—is hard to find now. Less and less detail is applied to a new house, and so it is up to homeowners to add their own personality. Luckily, more affordable plaster, paint, veneers, and MDF allow us to re-create our grander cousins at a reasonable price.

This living/dining room was ripe for a makeover, but the owners, Sylvie and Paul, had two problems. The first was a small budget and the second was Paul. He did not think there was anything wrong. Sylvie, however, felt it was time to move on: The home had been decorated by Paul's former partner.

Sylvie and I decided to address the more serious problem of cost. Although the dining room furnishings were dated, they were still in good condition, so instead of replacing them, we reinvented the suite. A frosted-glass pattern was applied to the glass doors of the buffet cabinet, and the top of the dining table was removed and replaced by a glass top with a metallic leaf pattern. The same metallic effect was applied to the coffee table. Simple canvas slipcovers were made for the straight-back chairs. The room was devoid of any ornamental detail, but we made it look bigger and heightened the ceiling by adding bold horizontal stripes in shades from taupe to khaki. A thin white line between the stripes helps pop the colors.

before

Typical living room and dining room decorated in the '80s with peach and gray walls, floral sofas in the same colors, and a pickled pine dining set.

Sylvie and Paul's living room sits open to their dining room and shares the upbeat horizontal-striped walls. To keep the light and airy feeling of the room, we used half-blinds in the recessed window, which allows for privacy but also lets in the sun. We repeated the metallic leafing technique on the glass-top coffee table and replaced their old sofas with a new one.

suburban update

"I wanted my rooms
to be up to date without
having to invest in a whole
new set of furnishings."

frosted glass doors

MATERIALS AND TOOLS

glass cleaner and paper towels

ruler or measuring tape

marker

low-tack painter's tape

scissors

self-adhesive shelf paper such as Con-Tact paper

soft, clean, lint-free rag

Frosted Glass Paint Kit (see Resources)

small roller and paint tray

small paintbrush

sharp knife (optional)

Pickled pine, hugely popular in the 1980s, can automatically date a room. To renew this cabinet, the wood was repainted and the glass doors were given a geometric design. The original wood surface was first roughed up with a light sanding, and high-adhesive primer was applied (follow the instructions in the preparation chapter, pages 162–63). We then applied 2 coats of off-white base coat. The same method was applied to the legs and sides of the dining room table. Although the size and shape of the cabinet cannot be changed, the piece is transformed by frosting the glass panels.

step 1 Place the glass door on a flat, sturdy work surface. Clean the glass and wipe dry.

step 2 **(Shot 1)** Measure the length and width of the glass and decide on your pattern. Here we have marked off evenly spaced squares with low-tack tape. (The squares will remain clear and the rest of the glass will be frosted.)

step 3 **(Shot 2)** Cut out squares from the Con-Tact paper that are the same size as the squares taped off on the glass. Remove the backing from the Con-Tact paper squares and stick them in position on the glass.

step 4 Remove the low-tack tape and press down on the Con-Tact paper squares again, using a soft, clean rag to make sure they are firmly stuck to the glass.

step 5 The Frosted Glass Paint Kit comes with a special formula to wipe over the surface to help the paint adhere. Apply according to the directions.

step 6 **(Shot 3)** Apply the frosted paint to the exposed glass with a small roller. Use a small brush to get in and around all the corners. Let dry for about 1 hour. If the coverage is uneven or not frosty enough, add a second coat. Let dry completely.

step 7 **(Shot 4)** Lift off the Con-Tact paper squares to reveal the clean glass underneath. A sharp knife will help lift the corners easily.

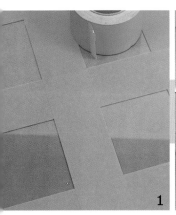

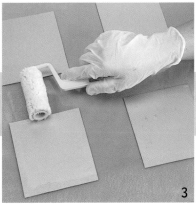
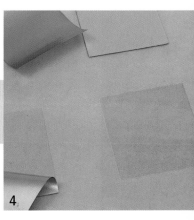

1   2   3   4

horizontal stripes

MATERIALS AND TOOLS

white latex paint, satin

roller and paint tray

pencil and ruler

chalk line

level

³/₄" low-tack painter's tape

4 shades of beige and/or green latex paint, ranging from dark to light, satin

Horizontal stripes may seem like an unorthodox choice, but they add dimension and interest to unadorned walls. Choose the 4 paint shades from the same color chip and paint them in order of dark to light down the wall.

Prepare your surface following the instructions in the preparation chapter, pages 162–63.

step 1   Apply 2 coats of white base coat and let dry for 4 hours or overnight.

step 2   Divide the wall into 4 equal parts. Use a chalk line and the level to create straight lines, then tape across the center of the line with the ³/₄" tape.

step 3   **(Shot 1)** Start at the top of the wall with the darkest color and apply 2 coats of each color—the darkest color may require 3 coats.

step 4   **(Shot 2)** Remove the tape carefully when the painting is complete, and let dry. You will have a ³/₄"-wide white stripe between each color.

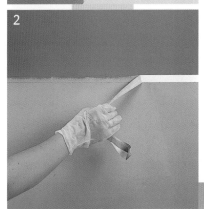

metallic leaf glass-top table

Like the cabinet, the pickled pine table was updated with a fresh coat of paint. To modernize the table, we removed the top and ran lengths of heavy-duty wire from opposing corners, secured with nautical clamps, to create a high-tech look and to maintain the table's stability. The highlight of this newly designed table is the pattern on the glass, which was produced with flakes of gold, green, and silver leaf. The wavy lines were made with a new type of masking tape designed to bend around curves. The metallic leaf was applied to the underside of the glass and sealed with several coats of clear varnish.

MATERIALS AND TOOLS

glass cleaner and paper towels

measuring tape

marker

masking tape

bendable masking tape

Aquasize (see Resources)

foam brush or roller

metallic leaf (we used gold, green, and silver; see Resources)

paper or plastic bag

natural bristle paintbrush

1″ artist's brush

plastic drop sheets

face mask

clear spray varnish

X-acto knife

step 1 Place the glass right side down onto a flat, sturdy surface. Clean the glass and wipe dry.

step 2 **(Shot 1)** Measure and mark, then mask off the area within which you are going to make your metallic design. We left a 4″ border around the rectangular tabletop. Then, using the bendable masking tape, create curving lines and waves down the length of the glass, taping inside and up to the masked-off perimeter. Press all the tape down firmly.

step 3 **(Shot 2)** Apply the Aquasize with a foam brush all over the exposed glass inside the border. It will go on milky and is ready when the surface has turned clear and is tacky to the touch.

step 4 **(Shot 3)** Rip the different colors of metallic leaf into pieces and mix them together in a paper or plastic bag.

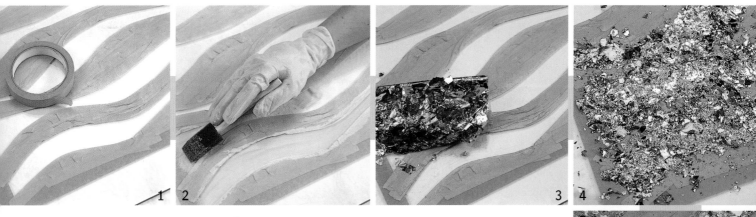

1

2

3

4

5

step 5 **(Shot 4)** Cover the sized area with the leaf mixture. Pat it down with your dry, clean fingers and a clean paintbrush. Let dry for ½ hour.

step 6 **(Shot 5)** Brush off the excess pieces with the artist's brush so that the surface is smooth and flat. Brush lightly in one direction to keep the excess from flying all over. (You can save these pieces for future projects.)

step 7 Attach plastic sheets to any exposed glass outside of the leafed area with masking tape. Put on a face mask, then spray the leafed area with clear varnish. Let dry to the touch (about 30 minutes) and spray again. Repeat 3 times.

step 8 **(Shot 6)** Using an X-acto knife, score all the edges of the tape so that when you lift the tape away from the glass it won't pull the varnish and metallic leaf away. Very carefully pull the tape back on itself to remove.

step 9 Carefully clean the glass, removing any residue of tape adhesive and scraping off any Aquasize or varnish that may have leaked under the tape.

step 10 **(Shot 7)** Mount the glass on the table.

6

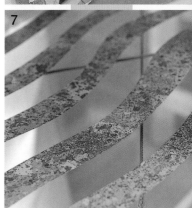

7

Layering textures throughout a room is a growing trend for modern interiors. A mixture of tactile surfaces is at its best when paired with earth colors, such as the warm tones of terra-cotta, raw umber, and burnt sienna; the soft pinks of raw plaster; and the cooler shades of chocolate, peat browns, heavy creams, and natural woods. Combining color and texture in a room can be achieved in many ways. First, you can mix texture and color simultaneously on a wall surface. Rub paint over a roughly plastered wall or polish a paint finish to a high sheen with a wax coating or a layer of high-gloss varnish. There are even paints that have the texture already mixed into them. Texture delights the senses and it can be played out in the furnishings: the cool softness of dark brown leather chairs, the coarseness of heavily woven sisal underfoot, the coziness of felt curtains, and the rough feel of natural woods.

"We needed a room that displayed our macho personalities but at the same time showed off our softer side."

Manny and Kevin are policemen. They have been best friends since childhood and are now roommates. They didn't think they had a problem with their apartment, but their girlfriends brought me into the picture. I wanted to keep the room masculine but make it stylish. The first thing we tackled were the walls—I took my inspiration from a Japanese shoji screen and divided the space into a grid of different-sized rectangles. Instead of using traditional latex paint, we applied a textured paint that gives the illusion and feel of soft suede. The pattern adds an extra dimension to the space. The original vertical blinds were replaced with lengths of coffee-colored felt, an inexpensive material that has a natural softness. By the time we had dressed the room with sumptuous leather furnishings our budget was getting rather tight, which often is the best way to get the imagination flowing. I picked up several waste paper baskets made from bleached wood. Two pairs were transformed into the legs of a console table, and the remainders were reinvented as atmosphere lighting. The guys (and their girlfriends) were thrilled with the results. It's a place where they feel equally comfortable entertaining their friends or flopping in front of the television with a bag of potato chips.

This is a rather dull room with low ceilings, old-fashioned venetian blinds, and spartan furniture.

rough&smooth

suede walls

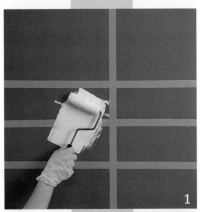

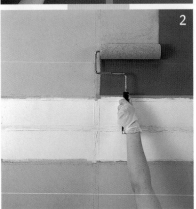

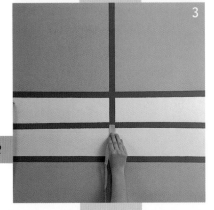

Several paint companies manufacture textured paint designed to create a more tactile surface than traditional paint and one of the most popular finishes is faux suede. You can make your own by adding an 8-ounce bag of silica sand to 1 gallon of latex paint. Mix extremely well and apply with a roller or brush. The effect looks and feels like soft suede.

step 1 Apply 2 coats of chocolate brown base coat and let dry for 4 hours or overnight.

step 2 Measure and mark off a grid that fits your wall measurements. Use the chalk line first, then check your work with the level. Our thin rectangles are 14" by 25" and the larger boxes are 25" by 50". Cover the chalk lines with the 1" low-tack tape. Press the edges down firmly.

step 3 **(Shot 1)** Fill in the long, thin rectangles with the cream paint.

step 4 Thoroughly mix the silica into the sand-colored paint.

step 5 **(Shot 2)** Fill in the large boxes with the textured paint. Let dry for 4 hours.

step 6 **(Shot 3)** Remove the tape carefully to reveal the dark base coat as the thin stripes. There is an interesting blend of rough and smooth textures on the wall.

console table

This ingenious table was built using wood waste-paper baskets as supports for a flat, hollow-core door. **(Shot 1)** Drill 4 holes into the base of each basket. To ensure that the holes are all in the same place on each base, measure down and in from each corner and mark the spot with a pencil. **(Shot 2)** Attach the baskets base to base with screws and washers. We painted the door chocolate brown and then applied 2 coats of high-gloss acrylic varnish for sheen and protection.

no-sew curtains

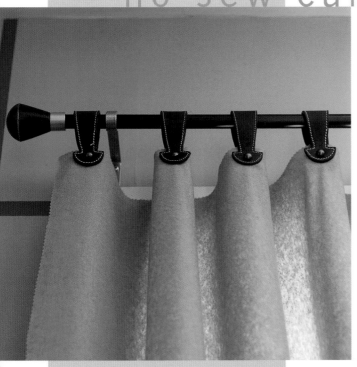

Luxury fabrics like camel hair and cashmere have become increasingly popular, but their cost can be prohibitive. A less expensive cousin is felt. Here, lengths of coffee-colored felt were used as curtains. No sewing was required, as pinking shears were used to cut the edges. The hanging loops are leather handles, reproductions of old trunk handles often used on modern furniture. Fold them into loops held together with upholstery tacks. You can cut small pieces of cork to cover the pin points at the backs of the straps.

Our awareness of the Far Eastern way of life has become more than just a passing interest. As we try to balance our busy lives, many of us are searching for an increasingly spiritual environment. *Chi* is the ancient Chinese concept of change through the flow of energy. *Yin* and *yang* are the expression of *chi* through alternating phases or opposites: light and dark, day and night, winter and summer. It is the interaction of yin and yang in your home that creates good *feng shui*, which is the art of living in harmony with your surroundings. If you plan to design a meditative space around this philosophy, there are many books and experts who will take you into great depth, but here are a few basic principles that will help. Furnishings with naturally flowing curves have a positive effect on the flow of energy, whereas hard angles are said to cause visual confusion. These angles can be broken with the placement of a plant, a mirror, or even lighting. A blend of different textures and a mix of mellow shades balanced with splashes of black or a touch of bright red will promote a feeling of peace and relaxation. Organic forms and water, either viewed through a window or incorporated into a room, are also important for an area that is calm, uncluttered, and serene. The bottom line to a harmonious space is, if it feels right to you, it probably is.

"I wanted to develop a meditative space where I could imagine unwinding and rejuvenating after work."

This is one of four model rooms we decorated for a home show; the others are featured on pages 32, 84, and 106. We began our journey into the creation of this serene living room with a collection of silk shantung pillows. The raw texture and delicate colors were then reproduced on the walls with paint. The main walls were divided into wide panels, and the fireplace wall was divided into eight squares—a lucky number in *feng shui* design. These squares were then decorated with Chinese symbols meaning peace and tranquillity. Newly built homes come with a large selection of prefinished hardwood floors. To enhance this floor, we painted a carpet directly over the top using the same symbols. The gentle curves of the furnishings, such as the yin and yang coffee table, set up a harmonious balance. Although pewter is a strong color, its earthiness is soothing, and I used paint on the fireplace to replicate the finish on the table. The crowning touch for a tranquil room is water. It could be a simple glass bowl with floating candles, or one of the many indoor fountains designed for this purpose.

now & zen

faux silk wall panels

There is nothing as delicate as raw silk, and yet it has an integral strength that suits the meditative qualities of this living room. To reproduce the look of silk on the walls, I applied a metallic glaze over the soft pastel–colored panels. Metallic paints work best in rooms where either natural or artificial light can dance off this slightly reflective surface. For the glaze, I mixed gold and white metallic paints together and then added this mixture to glazing liquid. The colored glaze was then rolled over the panels and dragged with a brush horizontally and vertically to create the lines of silk fabric weave. Each square was then hand-painted with the Chinese characters depicting peace and tranquillity.

MATERIALS AND TOOLS

chalk line

4 pastel colors (gray, sand, green, mauve) latex paint, semigloss

3" paintbrush

rollers and paint trays

low-tack painter's tape

pencil, measuring tape, and ruler

antique silver and white metallic latex paint

mixing containers

water-based glazing liquid

paint mixing stick

dragging brush or household scrub brush

photocopied image

Mylar, marker, and X-acto knife

spray adhesive

pewter metallic paint

artist's brush

RECIPE

1 part antique silver–and–white metallic paint mixture

4 parts water-based glazing liquid

Prepare your surface following the instructions in the preparation chapter, pages 162–63.

step 1   After the walls have been primed, use the chalk line to divide 1 wall into large, equal squares.

step 2   Apply a base coat of a different color to each square. Paint every other square and when those are dry, fill in the remaining ones. You may mask off the squares with low-tack tape if you don't feel comfortable painting along the edges.

step 3   In the center of each pastel panel, with pencil and ruler mark and mask off a 4" square with low-tack tape.

step 4   Thoroughly mix 1 part antique silver with 1 part white metallic paint. Mix a colored glaze according to the recipe.

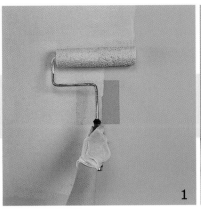

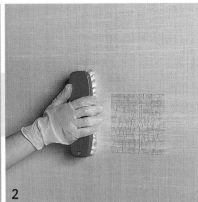

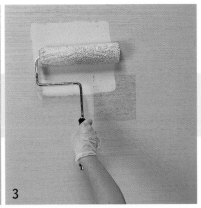

1 | 2 | 3

step 5   **(Shot 1)** Working on one panel at a time, roll on the colored glaze.

step 6   **(Shot 2)** Pull a dragging brush horizontally across the square through the glaze. Wipe excess glaze off the brush after each pull. To allow a clean line between the different squares, drag alternating squares, let them dry, and then drag the rest of the squares and let them dry.

step 7   **(Shots 3 and 4)** Working on one panel at a time, roll on a second coat of colored glaze and pull the dragging brush through the glaze vertically in one long stroke, creating a fine weave in the paint. Wipe excess glaze off the brush after each pull. Let dry.

step 8   Remove the tape from the 4″ squares to reveal the base coat.

step 9   Photocopy your chosen motif to fit inside the 4″ squares. Lay a sheet of Mylar over your design and trace it using a marker. Cut out the design with an X-acto knife.

step 10   **(Shot 5)** Spray the stencil with some adhesive and press it into place in the 4″ square, making sure the design is centered. Draw around the stencil with a pencil, transferring the design to the square.

step 11   **(Shot 6)** Remove the stencil, and fill in the design with pewter metallic paint, using an artist's brush.

4

5 | 6

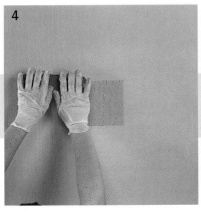

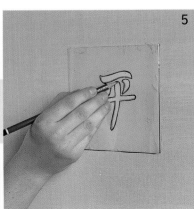

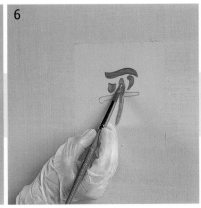

pewter fireplace

MATERIALS AND TOOLS

black latex paint, satin

roller and paint tray

gray metallic paint

soft, clean, lint-free rags

artist's molding paste or ornamental gesso

1 tablespoon aluminum powder

face mask

spatula

stiff bristle paintbrush

fretwork stencil

RECIPE

2 cups artist's molding paste or gesso

1 teaspoon black latex paint

1 tablespoon aluminum powder

Note: This is not a working fireplace. We do not recommend painting the inside of the firebox in a working fireplace.

Note: Never use paint or artist's plaster inside the firebox of a working fireplace.

Pewter's wonderful finish adds an interesting element to the Zen-like atmosphere. The fireplace surround was given a base coat of black and then lightly rubbed with a gray metallic paint. The inside of the box was decorated with a stencil using tinted plaster to produce a raised design, which you can only do in a non-working fireplace.

Prepare your surface following the instructions in the preparation chapter, pages 162–63.

step 1 Apply 2 coats of black base coat to the surround and firebox and let dry for 4 hours.

step 2 **(Shot 1)** For the surround, rag on the gray metallic paint over the black base coat, creating the soft, cloudy appearance of pewter.

step 3 **(Shot 2)** Tint the paste according to the recipe. Adjust the color to suit by matching it with the pewter-colored surround. Always wear a face mask when handling and mixing powders, as they are toxic and become airborne. Apply a skim coat of the paste with a spatula to the inside of the firebox, and pounce the surface lightly with a stiff paintbrush to even out the texture. Let it set for a few hours, then rub a spatula over the surface to remove any peaks.

 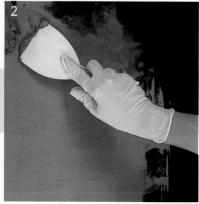

painted carpet

MATERIALS AND TOOLS

low-tack painter's tape

sandpaper

high-adhesion primer

light and dark gray latex paint, satin

roller with extension handle and tray

water-based glazing liquid

mixing container

household bristle brush

pencil

*antique white and medium gray paint,
    latex*

artist's brush

acrylic varnish

varnish brush or foam brush

RECIPE

1 part dark gray latex paint

1 part water-based glazing liquid

Styling your own painted carpet gives you the freedom to incorporate special motifs, colors, and themes from elsewhere in the room. A carpet painted directly onto a hardwood floor can also be the finishing touch in a contemporary setting. Here two tones of gray were painted to resemble the texture of a heavy weave and then Chinese characters were hand painted in an oriental pattern.

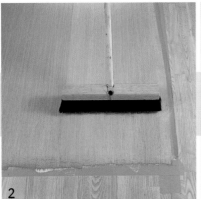

Note: This carpet was applied over a hardwood floor that had been sealed and varnished. You must first sand the faux carpet area to rough up the varnish and clean it well with a strong cleanser. Then use a high-adhesion primer to ensure your new paint finish will stand up to traffic. Prepare your surface following the instructions in the preparation chapter, pages 162–63.

step 1 **(Shot 1)** Mark off an area on your hardwood floor with low-tack tape in the shape of a rug. Press down firmly to avoid leakage. Lightly sand and prime the taped-off area. Apply 2 coats of light gray base coat. Let dry for 4 hours.

step 2 **(Shot 2)** Mix the dark gray glaze. Apply it over the light gray base coat with a roller, covering the surface completely. Drag a hard bristle brush through the wet glaze, creating lines like fabric weave. Let dry for 4 hours.

step 3 **(Shot 3)** Draw a design on the rug with a pencil. Paint it in freehand with an artist's brush and antique white paint.

step 4 **(Step 4)** To make the fringe, start by painting in the fringe shadows with medium gray paint, and then paint white fringe over the top. Let dry overnight.

step 5 Apply 4 or 5 coats of varnish with a varnish brush to protect your work.

traditional rooms

Rooms that are decorated in a traditional way are often time-honored places, where we afford ourselves the pleasure of loving yesterday today. There is much to see, enjoy, and remember in an atmosphere robust with color and softened with age. The furnishings may be a bit of a jumble: inherited pieces that have been restuffed and re-covered, one or two well-worn but polished antiques, yard-sale items that have been cleaned up and reinvented for your needs. New acquisitions will always work well, fitting comfortably alongside dark wood, rich patterns, and trimmings. In keeping with traditional styles, displays are the rule, not the exception. Fill a side table with a collection of framed photographs; line a glass-front buffet with the family china; group candlesticks together on the mantel or dining room table; pile a selection of favorite books beside the couch. These keepsakes and mementos are meant to be cherished. Paint finishes hold pride of place in a traditional room, whether English, French, or American, and make a fresh alternative to wallpapers. You can apply colored glazes to build up drama, depth, and history, as they allow us to use strong colors without the heaviness of a solid surface of opaque paint. Aged finishes will transform new or found objects into tomorrow's antiques.

The grand homes of the Georgian period (1700–1830) had splendid exteriors and very grand interiors. Synonymous with eighteenth-century England, this "golden age" of architecture encompasses many different styles, from Palladian, Rococo, Neoclassic, and Regency in Europe to Colonial and then Federal in America. Although Georgian style varied throughout the century, these homes, whether in America or Europe, share a sense of elegance and a remarkable attention to detail. Architects and designers today still take inspiration from this period, although the great craftsmanship of the eighteenth century is sadly no longer affordable or even available. The Georgians relished decorative walls, from painted faux marble, influenced by the grand interiors of Italy, to ornate plasterwork and paneling. Later, elaborate hand-painted wallpapers came into force. Color was also rich and sumptuous, often accented with flat white.

"I love beautiful things, and collect

Georgian-style antiques and interesting artworks.

Now I want this room to reflect my taste."

After I showed the owner, Sam, a gorgeous book on the extravagance of Georgian style and explained how it suited his possessions, he was hooked. We took our cue from the era's passion for rich tones and ornamentation and layered the living room with detail. A frieze was created around the room by adding stock trim and decorative moldings to the minimal crown molding that was already there. The plain white walls were given a yellow ocher paint treatment that replicates lightly creased paper. To live up to the full promise of Georgian style, the room needed a fireplace as a focal point. Budget concerns restricted us to simply making a mantel and surround of MDF with a trompe l'oeil screen and hearth. Obviously, the fireplace cannot be used, but the illusion is dramatic. The final touch was to swag dramatic Regency-style crimson curtains in the window. This glorious Georgian-style living room is now a favorite gathering place for Sam and his friends, and a place where he can relax and enjoy his beloved collections.

before

The owner of this Victorian home built circa 1900 has spent the last seven years doing basic fix-ups. The living room is on a grand scale, but it had no fireplace, which is unusual for this period.

georgian
living room

creased walls

MATERIALS AND TOOLS

off-white and yellow ocher latex paint, satin

rollers and trays

low-tack painter's tape

water-based glazing liquid

mixing container

3″ paintbrush

soft, clean, lint-free rags

RECIPE

1 part yellow ocher latex paint

2 parts water-based glazing liquid

This is a marvelous technique, especially if you are working on old walls, or even new walls that need character. The various shades and lines created as you play with the glaze produce great depth and texture while camouflaging any bumps and cracks.

Prepare your surface following the instructions in the preparation chapter, pages 162–63.

step 1 Apply 2 coats of off-white base coat and let dry for 4 hours or overnight.

step 2 Work on one wall at a time. With low-tack tape, mask off the baseboard, ceiling, and along the edges where the walls meet.

step 3 **(Shot 1)** Mix the yellow ocher glaze. Using the paintbrush, apply the glaze quite thickly to an area of about 4 square feet.

step 4 **(Shot 2)** Fold a rag so that it is fairly smooth. Rag the wall softly by dabbing over the wet glaze.

step 5 **(Shot 3)** Now push the glaze with the rag into creases or veins. Go back over the areas you have pushed to soften the white areas. The creases should have different intensities and lengths and go in various directions. Straight lines will not look realistic. Keep it random. Stand back and look at the overall effect you are making, and be sure you are not creating an even pattern.

step 6 Make sure to keep a wet edge (see page 159). Apply the glaze to the next section and continue creasing until the wall is finished. Let it dry for 4 hours or more depending on the glazing liquid. Then remove the tape along the edge of the unfinished wall edge and put it on the finished edge to ensure neat corners. Repeat the process on the remaining walls.

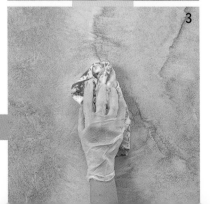

1

2

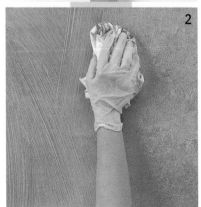

3

building a frieze

There is a huge selection of stock moldings available, and several companies also manufacture intricate and period-style moldings. When building a frieze, measure out the pattern and depth of the moldings in proportion to your room. Miter the corners for a professional finish, and adhere the molding strips to the walls with wood glue and small nails. Apply 2 coats of white paint to all the components of the frieze to unify the design.

MATERIALS AND TOOLS

urn and swag wood ornaments

dentil molding

primer

1" paintbrush or foam brush

measuring tape

pencil

low-tack painter's tape

wood glue

finishing nails

hammer

white latex paint, semigloss

2" paintbrush

step 1 Prime the wood ornaments.

step 2 Decide on the width of the frieze (between 12 and 16 inches). Tape the section off and then prime it. (On our wall, there was already a cove molding in place, which is part of the frieze.)

step 3 **(Shot 1)** The ornaments should be centered in the frieze. Use a measuring tape and pencil to mark out the positions. A helpful trick is to apply a bit of low-tack painter's tape to the ornaments and stick them up, moving them around until they look right.

step 4 **(Shot 2)** Remove the ornaments one at a time, apply glue to the backs, and place them back into position. Secure each ornament with one or two finishing nails.

step 5 **(Shot 3)** Cut the dentil molding to the length of the wall, prime it and when dry attach it to the bottom of the frieze with glue and finishing nails.

step 6 **(Shot 4)** Apply two coats of white semigloss paint to the frieze.

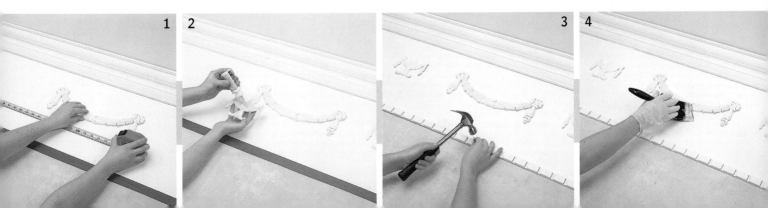

faux marble fireplace

It is not as difficult as it may seem to make your own fireplace surround. First, decide on its size—the height, width, and depth that fit the dimensions of your room. Measure and tape the shape to your wall to make sure the proportions are right. We built a plain shape from MDF, cutting 2 sides, a front, and a mantel. Once nailed together, the facade was primed and 2 coats of white semigloss paint were applied as the base coat. To dress up the surround we painted faux Sienna marble panels on the front and then added stock molding. A faux hearth was cut from MDF, and the grout lines were carved out using a router, but you could tape off and then paint in grout lines. Once the MDF was painted in mottled stone colors, the effect was very convincing. The fire screen was also cut from MDF, and a hand-painted Georgian-style urn embellishes the sumptuous look. The ornate plasterwork and white paint are typical of the Georgian period and look just as splendid in this Victorian living room.

MATERIALS AND TOOLS

white latex paint, semigloss

small roller and paint tray

low-tack painter's tape

burnt sienna, burnt umber, and raw sienna artist's acrylic paint

water-based glazing liquid

mixing containers

3 small paintbrushes, 1½"–2" wide

soft cotton rags

badger-hair or soft bristle paintbrush

black watercolor crayon

water

high-gloss acrylic varnish

foam brush

RECIPE

1 part artist's acrylic paint

1 part water-based glazing liquid

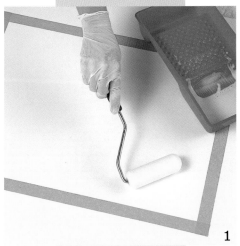

1

2

3

4

For a realistic-looking marble, find a picture of a real piece and try to copy the direction and intensity of the veins. Artist's acrylics give a more authentic color to your work. Prepare your surface following the instructions in the preparation chapter, pages 162–63.

step 1 **(Shot 1)** Apply 2 coats of white base coat to the surface and let dry for 4 hours. Work in panels to give the effect of real marble. Mask off the panels with low-tack tape.

step 2 **(Shot 2)** Mix 3 colored glazes according to the recipe, using the burnt sienna, burnt umber, and raw sienna artist's acrylics. Apply the glazes with the 2″ paintbrushes in random patches, filling in the entire panel.

step 3 **(Shot 3)** Blend and soften the colors with a rag or soft bristle brush. Add more color where necessary, and if your glazes are drying out, apply some glazing liquid over the top.

step 4 **(Shot 4)** Use the watercolor crayon to make the veins. Make sure that you always keep the crayon wet so that it flows properly. Create a crooked line starting or ending at a panel edge. Go back to the top of the line and create jagged disks down the line. Wrap a rag around the end of your finger and wipe away the glaze from inside the disks. Use the soft bristle brush to soften the lines and blend them into the background marble.

step 5 Let the panel dry and then retape and start the next panel. To save time, work on alternate panels. Don't tape over fresh paint until it has had sufficient time to dry and always use low-tack tape.

step 6 Once all the panels are finished and dry, apply 2 coats of high-gloss varnish for sheen and protection.

georgian dining

Georgians relished bold dark colors, which suited the habit of lavish entertaining. The most popular color was red, because of its powers to stimulate the appetite and conversation, and to flatter skin tones. When combined with candlelight bouncing off glassware and heavily polished surfaces, the effect is magical. For this dining room I chose a reddish coral, which is surprisingly soothing by day but vibrant in the evening. A flat latex paint was used to camouflage the condition of the bumpy, uneven plaster walls. To highlight the dramatic color, I decoupaged wallpaper trim to border oversized panels around the room. This architectural trick is a great solution to bring a large wall into scale with the size of the room, and was applied in most grand Georgian homes, although their craftsmen used plaster trim. Sam was delighted with the way the walls enhanced his antique furnishings and complemented his Georgian-style living room.

decoupage
panels

You can choose any inexpensive wallpaper border to create these panels. The idea is to reinvent the design of the wallpaper border with a pair of scissors. **(Shot 1)** Keep the part of the design you like and cut away the rest. Change the proportions of the border and the pattern layout to fit your own specifications. **(Shot 2)** Apply the paper strips to the wall with wallpaper glue and use sharp scissors or an X-acto knife to cut mitered corners for a neat finish. Wash any glue from the walls. The decoupage does not require varnish, but it will protect the paper if you wish to wash the walls down at a later date.

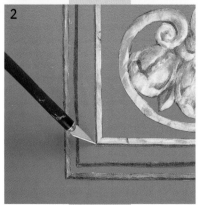

I grew up in the quintessential English home—a noisy place full of children and dogs. And, of course, a fabulous garden. In fact, it was the garden that received most of the attention. The decoration of the house just seemed to evolve. The living room was the place where we all gathered; English homes rarely have basements. It was filled with oversized sofas, usually with a sleeping dog on one of them, a roaring fire to burn off the damp English air, and antiques and family mementos that had been handed down for generations. English style, especially rural living, is a little like its inhabitants—comfortable, well worn, with a touch of eccentric elegance and whimsy. It is an uncomplicated look that evolves within a home over time as a family grows and lives in the house. These simple ingredients will give a room a relaxed elegance and make it a room that can be and is lived in.

"I wanted my family to use this room, to gather and feel comfortable here with all our friends, as well as a place where I could curl up and read by the fire."

Judy's living room had all the basic features that make you feel right at home, but it lacked the right backdrop. Color was the first solution to warming up the room. Silk damask was a popular wall covering in grand English homes at the beginning of the nineteenth century before the production and popularity of manufactured wallpapers. Although beautiful, the fabric was so delicate that the sun badly faded and weakened it over time. I wanted to re-create its transparent patterns, so I used diluted paint over a giant damask stencil. The crimson walls are rich but not heavy and are highlighted with a cream-colored ceiling and dove gray cove molding. Judy's fireplace is common to homes built in the 1930s. The brick is not of the best quality, and the mantel is cut from a low-grade wood. By turning the mantel into a crown mantel and plastering the front, the fireplace is now a grand focal point to the room. The furnishings were rearranged and thinned out to make a warm, cozy space that everyone enjoys, including the dog.

before

All the elements were here, but the formal layout and drab green walls meant that this uninviting room was rarely used.

english
living room

damask stenciled walls

These walls appear to be covered in a rich but slightly faded damask silk, but in fact it is paint. You need a large stencil for the job, and use a roller or a large soft bristle brush to speed up the process. It's important to center your pattern, so pick a central point (such as over the fireplace) and begin there. To lighten the effect and give the illusion of sheer fabric, a glaze in the same color as the stencil was dragged over the surface.

MATERIALS AND TOOLS

light cream, dark and medium red latex paint, satin

rollers and paint tray

damask wallpaper stencil (see Resources)

pencil and measuring tape

spray adhesive

level

3" or 4" soft bristle brush (for stenciling)

paper towels

water-based glazing liquid

mixing container

wide bristle brush

RECIPE

1 part medium red latex paint

3 parts water

Prepare your surface following the instructions in the preparation chapter, pages 162–63.

step 1 Apply 2 coats of cream base coat and let dry for 4 hours.

step 2 Using the damask stencil as your guide, measure out where it will go on the wall and fill in the registration marks with pencil to place it properly. Start measuring from a central point, such as over the fireplace or the center of the wall, and move along from there.

step 3 (Shot 1) Spray the back of the stencil with adhesive and position it over the registration marks on the wall. Use the level to make sure it is straight. Fill in the stencil with the dark red paint. Dip a large soft brush into the paint, rub most of the paint off the bristles onto a paper towel, and dry-brush the paint over the stencil. Remove the stencil carefully, and reposition it using the registration marks to guide you. Continue until all the walls are stenciled.

step 4 (Shot 2) To make the stenciled walls look softer and silkier, first apply a thin layer of glazing liquid to the wall with a roller. Then dilute the medium red paint with water

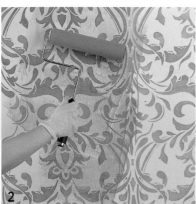

according to the recipe. Working in an area of about 4 square feet, apply the thinned-down paint over the glaze.

step 5 **(Shot 3)** Use the wide bristle brush to push through the wet paint vertically and horizontally to create the look of fabric weave. Some areas should be lighter and some darker. Work randomly over the stenciled wall. This will give the pattern the illusion that it was printed on sheer fabric.

step 6 **(Shot 4)** Getting perfect edges where the walls meet is difficult with a large stencil, especially on old, uneven walls. In this room, I painted a semisheer strip along the top and down each edge using 1 part paint to 1 part glaze. You can still see the stencil pattern, but any imperfections are now blurred.

fireplace

To improve the look of the fireplace, I applied layers of pretinted black cement over the brick area until I had a smooth surface, and then rubbed charcoal glaze over the top to give depth to the finish. I transformed the original mantel by adding a piece of wood around the base, creating a crown mantel, and finished it in a slightly lighter tone of gray.

The classic English dining room is typically handsome, with a formal atmosphere. It's steeped in a history of heavy furniture polished to a high beeswax shine, gleaming ancestral silver, and fine china. But today's entertaining has become more relaxed and, quite frankly, much more fun. While the style remains classic, the traditional dark colors are being replaced with interesting jewel tones layered over metallic bases. These vibrant lush walls work just as well with the strong lines of antique furniture. The decoration needn't take itself too seriously, either. Soften up edges with hand-painted trims and borders, and choose patterns with a whimsical flavor.

"After wallpapering my dining room walls with a floral pattern, I knew I had made a terrible mistake."

Judy was so pleased with her living room makeover (see page 72) that there was no stopping her as the two of us attacked her dining room. The first big job was to remove the floral wallpaper, and immediately the beauty of her Victorian home and furnishings began to talk to us. Once the paper was off the walls, we were left with plaster moldings framing large panels. Instead of downplaying the moldings, as the wallpaper did, we made them a statement with the clever use of paint. After applying a lustrous pearly metallic bronze base coat over the whole surface, I dragged a raspberry glaze over the top. Part of the challenge was to lighten up the room, and one of the ways to achieve this was to inject a sense of humor into the decor. I painted a haphazard gold border around the top of the room and at the top of each panel, and highlighted each plaster molding with brushstrokes of the gold paint. This whimsical touch was echoed on the back of the interior of the corner cabinets, where I painted rows of harlequin diamonds in deep ruby red and gold. As a grand finale, a valance box was built and then stenciled as a fitting crown for the velvet curtains. What a difference—the whole family agreed the room was magnificent!

The country wallpaper as a backdrop to the Victorian furnishings did nothing to enhance this dining room.

classic
dining room

textured walls

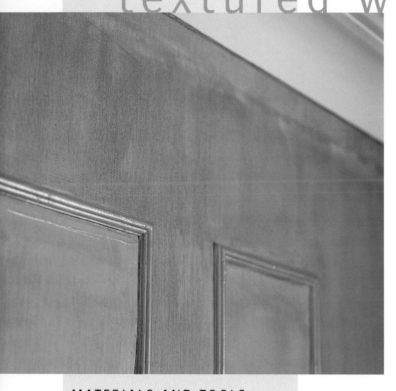

Premixed metallic paints are a new versatile tool for decorating. They can be used as a base coat under a colored glaze or mixed with glazing liquid and rubbed over a flat base coat. Both techniques will produce the rich, mellow hues of a metallic finish. I added an uneven gold border to these walls to keep the mood light and fun.

MATERIALS AND TOOLS

white latex paint, satin
roller and paint tray
metallic bronze paint
water-based glazing liquid
mixing containers
thick 3" wide bristle brush
raspberry latex paint, satin
small foam roller and paint tray
denim tool or stiff bristle brush
metallic gold and darker yellow gold
  latex paint
2" paintbrush

RECIPES

1 part bronze metallic paint
1 part water-based glazing liquid

1 part raspberry latex paint
1 part water-based glazing liquid
1 part water

2 parts dark gold latex paint
1 part water-based glazing liquid

Prepare your surface following the instructions in the preparation chapter, pages 162–63.

step 1 Apply 2 coats of white base coat and let dry for 4 hours.

step 2 **(Shot 1)** Mix the bronze metallic glaze and apply it with a wide brush, covering the wall surface completely and pulling the brush through the glaze in straight vertical lines. Let dry completely.

step 3 **(Shot 2)** Mix the raspberry glaze. This glaze is very thin, so apply it with the foam roller. Leave a 2" band of bronze along the top of the wall for a border. Don't use tape, as the line is supposed to be uneven and blurry.

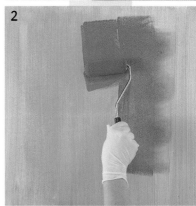

step 4 **(Shot 3)** Pull the denim tool through the glaze vertically, cleaning the excess glaze from the bristles as you go. The more you play with it, the more the bronze base will show through. If it starts to dry, roll on more raspberry glaze with the roller.

step 5 Apply metallic gold paint along the border that was left free of raspberry glaze. Paint it on freehand and overlap the raspberry slightly.

step 6 **(Shot 4)** Mix the darker yellow gold glaze and apply it over the metallic gold border.

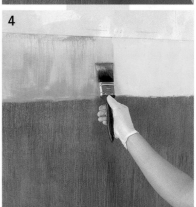

step 7 **(Shot 5)** Immediately follow with the denim tool, pulling through the gold glaze vertically to create the same kind of striated look that the raspberry walls have.

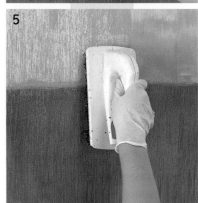

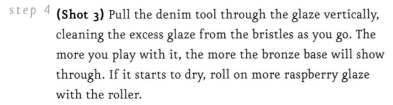

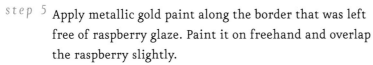

harlequin diamond
corner cabinet

MATERIALS AND TOOLS

medium and ruby red and gold latex paint, satin

2″ paintbrush

small foam roller and paint tray

marker and ruler

Mylar

X-acto knife

spray adhesive

low-tack painter's tape

paper towels

Harlequin patterns have been used throughout history to inject a bit of humor to an area of a room or a piece of furniture. Judy's corner cabinet was the ideal place to paint a harlequin backdrop to display her favorite china.

step 1 Remove the shelves from the cabinet. Prepare your surfaces following the instructions in the preparation chapter, pages 162–63. Apply 2 coats of medium red base coat to the inside walls. Let dry for 4 hours.

step 2 To make the diamond stencil, with a marker and ruler draw 5 elongated diamonds of equal size, midpoints touching, onto a sheet of Mylar. Cut out every other diamond with an X-acto knife.

step 3 **(Shot 1)** Position the stencil above the line where the shelves will be. Use spray adhesive as well as low-tack tape to hold the stencil firmly in place. Use a small foam roller to fill in the diamonds with ruby red paint. Dip the roller into the paint in the tray and then remove the excess onto a paper towel. Roll the paint over the diamond cutouts. Move the stencil along as you fill in all the red diamonds. Latex paint dries to the touch quickly, but make sure you don't press a stencil onto a wet diamond or it will smear the paint. Clean the stencil periodically to make sure there is no paint buildup on the back.

step 4 **(Shots 2 and 3)** Repeat the stenciling process for the alternating gold diamonds.

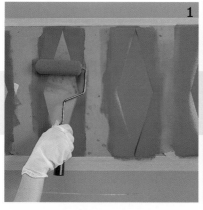 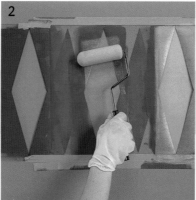 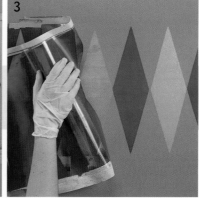

stenciled valance box

Although valances are not as popular given today's light and airy window treatments, one was needed to balance these richly colored walls and the heavy velvet curtains. This valance box was made with pieces of smooth plywood cut 6 inches wider than the width of the window and approximately 10 inches deep, but yours will depend on the size and height of your window. The front of the box was cut in a simple but ornate shape with a jigsaw. More elaborate decoration was added with a stencil. I frottaged the surface with a deep tone of ruby red over the raspberry base coat, which created the look of crushed velvet, and stenciled the pattern in antique gold.

MATERIALS AND TOOLS

wooden valance box

medium red and dark ruby red and gold latex paint, satin

water-based glazing liquid

mixing container

rollers and paint trays

sheets of white or brown paper large enough to cover the valance

cardboard the size of half the valance

pencil

sharp knife

low-tack painter's tape

sponge

paper towels

RECIPE

1 part dark ruby red latex paint

1 part water-based glazing liquid

Prepare your surface following the instructions in the preparation chapter, pages 162–63.

step 1 Apply 2 coats of medium red base coat to the valance box and let dry for 4 hours.

step 2 **(Shot 1)** To frottage the surface, mix the dark ruby red glaze and roll it onto the valance, covering the surface completely. Scrunch up the paper, open it up again, and lay the creased paper over the wet glaze. Flatten it down with your hands, then peel it off. The surface will now have a velvety texture. Let the surface dry completely before you stencil over it. Glazes differ in their drying time, but allow at least 4 hours.

step 3 **(Shot 2)** Make a cardboard stencil half the width of the valance. You will be flipping it so that the pattern is duplicated in reverse on the other half. Draw the design on the cardboard and cut it out. Secure the cardboard stencil onto the valance with low-tack tape (don't use spray adhesive on cardboard—it will not stick).

step 4 **(Shot 3)** Use a sponge and the gold paint to fill in the stencil. Dip the dampened sponge into the paint and remove the excess onto a paper towel. Dab the sponge over the cutout spaces, pressing the stencil down flat with your other hand. The sponge stenciling creates a lovely mottled effect.

step 5 Carefully remove the stencil. Make sure there is no wet paint on it before you flip it and tape it down to the other half of the valance. Fill in as in step 4. Let dry completely before attaching it to the window.

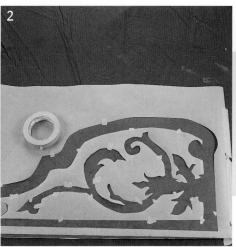
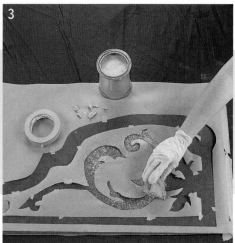

The function of a den is generally recreational; it's a place to read or play, listen to music or watch a movie. There is no greater luxury than having a separate space for these activities, and such a room should be designed around whatever makes you relax and brings your blood pressure down after a chaotic day. It could be tranquil pastels or, as in this case, rich metallics and an exotic atmosphere. When I started this project, I looked at the life and personality of Ernest Hemingway. A romantic and an adventurer, he was what is commonly called a man's man. I took inspiration for the wall decoration and the furnishings more from his lifestyle and personality than from any home he ever lived in. A dark, rich palette, a sexy fireplace, and a comfortable and adventurous cork floor are combined with oversized furnishings, which beg you to curl up in them with a drink and a good book, perhaps a copy of *For Whom the Bell Tolls.*

"The mission was to create a masculine room filled with robust colors and exotic finishes, where an adventurous spirit would feel at home."

This is one of four model rooms we decorated for a show house; the others are featured on pages 32, 54, and 106. Metallic paints have grown in popularity and are now a sophisticated finish used in many ingenious ways. Here I applied a bronze base coat, which if left alone looks garish, but by roughly ragging dark brown glaze over the top, the bronze peeks through, catching the light and adding drama to an otherwise very ordinary space. The room had no ceiling molding, so I created detail with a line of upholstery studs that finish the walls like a piece of fine furniture. Walls this grand need to be paired with doors and trim of substance. This was achieved by applying bronze foil to their surfaces. The striking floor pattern is made with cork, which is now available in a variety of colors. It's soft and warm underfoot, very durable, and you can design numerous patterns and inlays made to order. Deep leather club chairs are perfect to sink into, and the older they get, the more stylish they become. We treated the fireplace to a classic tortoiseshell finish. Artists have been imitating this rare material for centuries. It looks best if you use it on small areas, such as trinket boxes, candleholders, and, as we have done here, replicating the look of real tortoiseshell inlays. All the men who saw this room loved it, but then, that was the idea.

hemingway
den

stippled bronze walls

MATERIALS AND TOOLS

metallic bronze and dark brown latex paint, semigloss

rollers and paint trays

water-based glazing liquid

mixing container

stippling brush or wide, flat bristle paintbrush

paper towels or rags

measuring tape

chalk and chalk line

³/₄″ upholstery studs

hammer

RECIPE

1 part dark brown latex paint

4 parts water-based glazing liquid

Metallic paints are wonderful for creating dramatic wall finishes but can be garish if left alone. A translucent, colored-glaze top coat makes all the difference. It is roughly ragged over the surface so that the bronze base coat glows through.

Prepare your surface following the instructions in the preparation chapter, pages 162–63.

step 1 Apply 2 coats of metallic bronze base coat and let dry for 4 hours.

step 2 **(Shot 1)** Mix the dark brown glaze and roll it over the bronze base coat. Working in sections, apply the colored glaze and then pounce over the glaze with the stippling brush. Periodically, use a paper towel or rag to remove the wet glaze from the bristles of the brush. Play with this technique until you see the bronze base coat showing through, and there are lighter and darker areas. Let dry.

step 3 **(Shot 2)** Measure and mark approximately 18″ down from the ceiling and make a chalk line across the wall. Measure along this line and mark a spot every 6″.

step 4 **(Shot 3)** Tap in the studs over the marks. Wipe off the chalk marks.

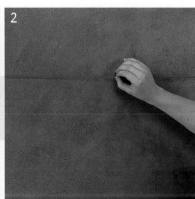

foil door

An inexpensive, lightweight hollow-core door was made to look like a heavy metal one. The grandiose effect is created with metallic transfer paper, which is relatively new on the market and great fun to work with. The surface should be painted a tone of the color of the metallic paper you are using. To diminish some of the garishness of the bright bronze transfer paper, a dark brown glaze was rubbed over the surface, and a coat of varnish was applied to protect the finish.

MATERIALS AND TOOLS

bronze latex paint, semigloss
small roller and paint tray
Aquasize (see Resources)
3″ paintbrush
bronze metallic transfers (see Resources)
soft, clean, lint-free rags
dark brown latex paint, flat or satin
water-based glazing liquid
mixing container
semigloss acrylic varnish
foam brush

RECIPE

1 part dark brown latex paint
4 parts water-based glazing liquid

Prepare your surface following the instructions in the preparation chapter, pages 162–63.

step 1 Apply 2 coats of bronze base coat to the door and let dry for 4 hours.

step 2 **(Shot 1)** Brush on 1 coat of Aquasize, wait 10 minutes, and then apply a second coat. It goes on milky and is dry when it turns clear, in about 10 minutes. But it will still feel tacky to the touch.

step 3 **(Shot 2)** Lay a sheet of metallic transfer onto the door shiny side up and rub firmly with a soft, clean rag. Don't use your fingers, as they will leave prints on the transfer.

step 4 Peel the outer plastic backing away and the bronze will have transferred onto the door. Reapply where needed. The surface will look distressed and you will see a bit of the bronze base coat showing through in spots.

step 5 **(Shot 3)** Mix the dark brown glaze and rub it over the door with a rag to take down the metallic shine and create a more aged surface appearance. Apply 2 coats of semigloss varnish to add sheen and to protect your work.

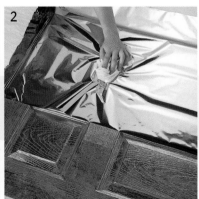

cork floor

Cork has been used as flooring in Europe for many years but is just beginning to become popular in North America. Cork floors are extremely durable, can be stained to any color, and can be installed already sealed. Cork is an environmentally friendly product, as it is produced from the bark of the cork oak tree grown across Portugal. The bark is stripped, but the tree is left standing, and the bark grows back within 9 years. Cork flooring is reasonably priced and is traditionally used in kitchens and bathrooms, but with today's elaborate patterns it is showing up in any room in the home.

faux tortoiseshell fireplace

A simple box fireplace surround was given a magical makeover with small inlays of faux tortoiseshell. Not difficult to produce, the brown and black tones are rich and exotic and turn a bland piece into a very special focal point. Faux tortoiseshell should always have several coats of high-gloss varnish to replicate the beauty of the real thing.

MATERIALS AND TOOLS

low-tack painter's tape

mid-brown and dark brown latex paint,
 satin

3" paintbrush

water-based glazing liquid

mixing container

small roller and paint tray

soft, clean, lint-free rags

flogger or thick long-hair bristle brush

paper towels

golden yellow latex paint, semigloss

2" foam brush

raw sienna, burnt sienna, and burnt
 umber artist's acrylic paint

plastic plate

1" artist's brush

badger-hair or soft bristle brush

artist's brushes

high-gloss acrylic varnish

foam brush

RECIPE

4 parts water-based glazing liquid

1 part dark brown latex paint

Faux Tortoiseshell Fireplace Continued

For the fireplace surround:

Tape off the area where you want the tortoiseshell panels to go. Paint the rest of the surround as follows.

step 1 Apply 2 coats of mid-brown base coat and let dry 2 to 4 hours.

step 2 Mix the dark brown glaze and roll it over the base coat.

step 3 Dab the glaze with a rag very softly to break up the surface slightly. Immediately pull the flogger softly through the glaze, always working in one direction. Wipe excess glaze off the bristles onto a paper towel as you go along. Let dry.

For the tortoiseshell panels:

Note: After the yellow base coat has been applied to the area where the tortoiseshell design is going to be, mask off the panels with low-tack tape and paint the design on every other one. When dry, reverse the tape and paint the remaining panels.

step 1 Apply 2 coats of golden yellow base coat and let dry for 4 hours.

step 2 After taping off the small panels, put small amounts of the 3 artist's acrylics onto a plastic plate.

step 3 **(Shot 1)** Working on one panel at a time, apply 1 coat of clear water-based glazing liquid over the yellow base coat.

step 4 **(Shot 2)** Immediately, while the glaze is still wet, brush the raw sienna over the surface with a 1" artist's brush in random patches.

step 5 **(Shot 3)** Next, brush the burnt sienna in scattered patches smaller than the raw sienna patches. Finally, brush on very small random patches of the burnt umber.

step 6 **(Shot 4)** Hold the badger-hair brush at right angles and gently brush over the colors, working in one direction. This gently blurs the colors and removes the brushstrokes. Let dry for a few hours depending on the glazing liquid used.

step 7 **(Shot 5)** Dip an artist's brush into burnt umber mixed with a bit of water. Spatter the paint randomly over the surface. Soften again with the badger-hair brush.

step 8 When all the panels have been completed, remove the tape and apply 2 coats of high-gloss varnish. The sheen will add extra depth and definition to the faux tortoiseshell.

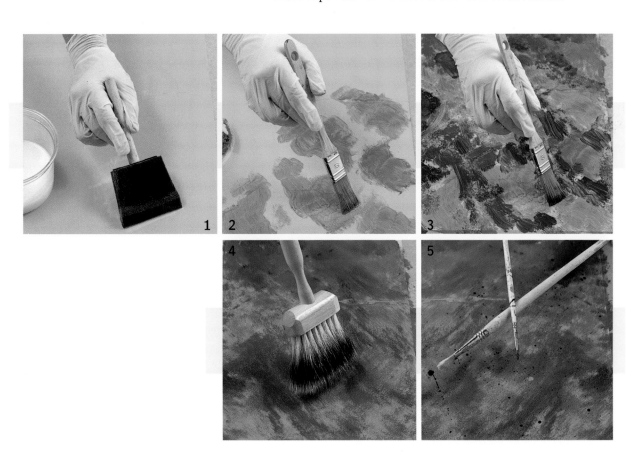

themed
rooms

An underlying theme permeates the decorating choices in these rooms. Whether you are building around a historical era that you love, a geographical location you have visited, the essence of your native country, or a storybook fantasy, the only rule is to work within the boundaries of that theme. You may already have a starting point in place, such as lengths of fabric and cushions, a carpet, a collection of china, ceramics, or silver, or a photo album overflowing with the colors and styles of your favorite holiday destination. Books, magazines, television, films, and travel offer endless resource material.

Furnishings do not have to be authentic but should share in the fantasy. Paint or plaster finishes will transform surfaces to suit whatever style you choose. Venetian plaster can be layered on in Mediterranean colors or drenched with the hot pastels of the islands. Stone floors and fireplaces are easily replicated with paint. Ethnic patterns, mosaic borders, and grassy walls will enrich the character in these imaginative spaces.

If you are unsure how to begin decorating, choosing a theme will act as a catalyst to fuel your imagination. You can take it as far as you please, or keep it light and subtle, but the room will always be interesting and a great conversation piece. All these rooms are statements about a time or place that is special to the homeowners.

The Elizabethans started the first building boom in England between the sixteenth and seventeenth centuries. At that time, due to international trading (and a great deal of looting), England was extremely prosperous. As the English traveled across Europe they became influenced by the grandeur they saw in countries like France and Spain. Back home they adapted the extravagant renaissance designs to their own English ideas of style. Much like today, the wealthy vied with their neighbors to see who could build bigger and more elaborate mansions. The original medieval manor houses built centuries earlier were constructed of wattle and daub, a traditional plaster and timber combination. The dining areas were in the great halls where the returning knights and their feudal lords not only ate but also slept. Gradually, the dining rooms moved from the drafty halls into what was known as the grand chamber. Entertaining became more civilized and the decor in these impressive rooms grew more refined. Many of the decorating words that we use today—cushion, ceiling, tapestry, chair—came from this fascinating period of design, from both the French and the English.

"Our collection of antique furniture is too grand

for our plain beige dining room."

Although this dining room sits in a home built in the 1980s, the homeowners' love of heavy oak antiques inspired me to have some fun with the decorating. Gail and Nico usually entertain on a lavish scale, and the plain beige room did nothing for a festive ambience. The only interesting feature in the room was the coffered ceiling, so I designed a ceiling with a blend of opulence and simplicity. You will often find elaborate tile on the ceilings of old English manor houses; this trick was used to bring their cavernous ceilings into proportion with the rooms. We used paint and stencils to imitate a medieval design, then applied a smoky wash over the top to simulate age. I hand-painted timber beams to match the existing oak woodwork and filled in the plaster area with a flat brick red paint. Candlelight was the order of the day in ancient Britain, so I found an iron chandelier for Gail and enhanced it with flickering bulbs. Romanced with masses of candles, jugs of wine, and great food, their dining room is ready for a party.

before

The house was built in the late 1980s when interior architectural details were dying out, but fortunately this dining room did have a coffered (or recessed) ceiling. The woodwork and door are unpainted oak, and the walls all beige.

elizabethan
dining room

painted tile ceiling

All rooms need a focal point, an interesting area that the eye is immediately drawn to. Coffered ceilings, although not incredibly decorative, do add an interesting dimension to a room, so I decided that this would be the special feature. We painted and stenciled a medieval design, which looks complicated but was relatively easy to do. However, periodic breaks to rest the neck muscles are required!

MATERIALS AND TOOLS

cream, red, blue, and medium gray latex paint, satin

roller with extension pole and paint tray

pencil and measuring tape

chalk line

Mylar, marker, and X-acto knife

spray adhesive

small foam rollers and paint trays

paper towels

ruler and black pencil crayon

water-based glazing liquid

mixing container

soft, clean, lint-free rangs

RECIPE

1 part medium gray latex paint

2 parts water-based glazing liquid

1 part water

Prepare your surface following the instructions in the preparation chapter, pages 162–63.

step 1 Apply 2 coats of cream base coat to the ceiling. For this job, do not use ceiling paint, as it is not as durable as regular latex. Let dry for 4 hours.

step 2 Measure the length and width of the ceiling and map it out to separate it into equal-sized squares. Use a chalk line to mark the grid. Each square is approximately 20″ x 20″.

step 3 Cut out a stencil from the Mylar the same size as the squares. Mark and cut out a square in the center, leaving about a 2½″ border all around the perimeter.

step 4 **(Shot 1)** Spray the back of the stencil with adhesive and press it into position on the ceiling. Load a foam roller with the red paint in the tray and roll off the excess on a paper towel. Fill in the cutout square with the roller. Remove the stencil and reposition, painting every other square red. Let the paint dry 2 to 4 hours.

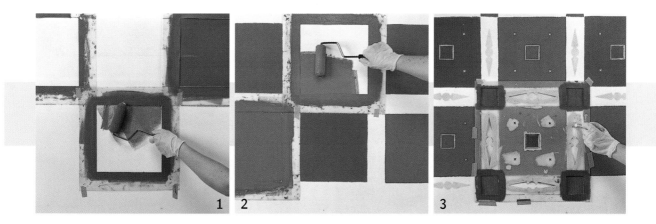

step 5 **(Shot 2)** Stencil all the other squares blue. Let dry 2 to 4 hours.

step 6 Cut out a second stencil, larger than the first, that will block the large square, and mark and cut a small square in each corner and some detail along the sides. (We also cut a small square in the center and outlined it with gray paint.)

step 7 **(Shot 3)** Spray the back of the stencil with adhesive and press it into position over the large red squares. Now paint all of the little corner squares in red and the side details in gray. Let dry 2 to 4 hours.

step 8 **(Shot 4)** Use a ruler and black pencil crayon to add arrows crossing the squares.

step 9 **(Shots 5 and 6)** Mix the gray glaze and apply it over the painted tiles quite thickly with a foam roller, working in 3′ patches. Dab and blend the surface with a rag to create a smoky, washed-out finish.

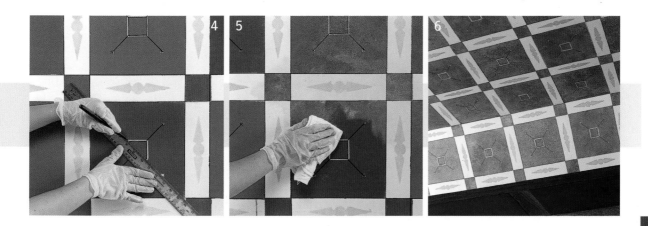

timber frame walls

Paint and a wood-graining tool are all that's required to replicate the sixteenth-century timber and plaster construction on these modern walls. Take a look at pictures of historic English houses and you will see plenty of interior and exterior designs that you can copy.

MATERIALS AND TOOLS

pencil and measuring tape

chalk line

golden honey and dark green-brown latex paint, satin

2″ paintbrush

water-based glazing liquid

mixing containers

foam brush

rocker (wood-graining tool)

paper towels

plastic stippling brush

brick red and medium gray latex paint, flat

3″ paintbrush

foam roller and paint tray

soft, clean, lint-free rags

light and dark brown artist's acrylic paint

artist's brush

Prepare your surface following the instructions in the preparation chapter, pages 162–63. For this project the primer is the base coat.

step 1 Measure and pencil in where you would like the wood timbers to go across, up and down, and diagonally on the wall. The timbers should be 4″–6″ wide.

step 2 With the 2″ paintbrush, hand-paint 2 coats of honey paint to the timbers.

step 3 **(Shot 1)** Mix the dark green-brown glaze. Working in single lengths, apply the glaze over the honey base with a foam brush.

step 4 **(Shot 2)** Pull the rocker through the wet glaze, rocking your wrist back and forth to create a wood-grain design. Clean the rocker with paper towels between strokes.

step 5 **(Shot 3)** Run the plastic stippling brush along the grain to soften the lines and break up the surface a bit. Let dry.

RECIPE FOR TIMBER GLAZE

1 part dark green-brown latex paint
1 part water-based glazing liquid

RECIPE FOR WALL GLAZE

1 part medium gray latex paint
2 parts water-based glazing liquid
1 part water

step 6 **(Shot 4)** Use the 3″ paintbrush to apply 2 coats of red paint to the wall space between the timbers. Don't tape off the timbers as the lines do not have to be perfectly clean; these are supposed to be old timbers. Do not use a roller for the walls as a brush will give a "period" look to the surface.

step 7 **(Shot 5)** Mix the gray glaze, and apply it over the red walls quite thickly with a foam roller, working in 3′ patches. Dab and blend the surface with a rag to create a smoky, washed-out finish.

step 8 **(Shot 6)** Apply shadows to the timbers with artist's acrylics, light brown on top and darker brown along the bottom. This will give the appearance that the timbers stand out slightly from the wall surface.

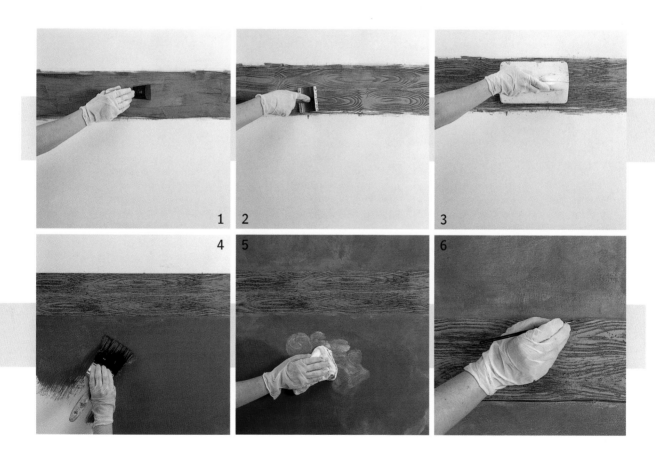

Traveling to far-off lands has become a standard vacation rather than pure luxury. Affordable package holidays have taken us to places we may only have dreamed of or seen on television or read about in books. On these travels we purchase thrilling mementos of our visit, but sometimes we return to discover that our beloved artifacts from Africa, Mexico, or Spain do not fit into our home's decor. It's a shame to tuck them away in a trunk or a spare bedroom, so why not invent a room around them. Create a backdrop that enhances your treasures and enables you to enjoy them every day. Sculptures, paintings, masks, jewelry, and even furniture need not be expensive and rare finds, but they are unusual and distinct in your own surroundings.

"My loft is spacious and I adore the treasures I've collected on my travels, but something was missing. I needed help."

Katherine's light and airy living space is one large room with two areas portioned off for the kitchen and bathroom. Her bed sits at one end of the oversized room. She did not want any more solid walls, but she did need a degree of privacy around the bedroom. The first thing I tackled was the placement of furniture. Very often the simple job of rearranging pieces automatically creates more space and a better flow throughout. Large panels of fabric would provide a privacy barrier, but the cost of the patterned material I looked at was beyond our budget. Instead, I bought a large roll of sheer muslin and tie-dyed an ethnic pattern using indigo dye. Once we had the fabric gently hanging in long sheets, the loft began to take on a breezy exotic spirit. We began to think of a romantic South Seas island. A wall design using the same indigo blue and pure white continued our fantasy. Blue radiates a natural energy and at the same time it is a peaceful and calm color; the white zigzag along the colorwashed walls balances the strong tones of the indigo and becomes an interesting backdrop for Katherine's collection of masks. The bathroom walls do not rise to the ceiling, creating an unattractive space. To solve the dilemma we secured pieces of wood, carved in seaweed shapes, along the top. This was inspired by the carved moldings seen in Indonesian homes that allow the air to circulate freely. The loft now has the timeless quality of a South Seas island: rich tones of the ocean and white sandy beaches sprinkled with driftwood. It's a never-ending vacation.

south seas loft

wavy wall

MATERIALS AND TOOLS

pencil

craft paper

scissors

spray adhesive

low-tack painter's tape

indigo blue latex paint, satin

water-based glazing liquid

mixing container

large paint tray

spongy floor mop or long-handled window washer

RECIPE

1 part indigo blue latex paint

1 part water-based glazing liquid

As a solid color, indigo would have been too heavy and dark for such a large wall, so we thinned down the paint with glaze and applied a colorwashed finish using long-handled window cleaners instead of paintbrushes to speed up the job.

Prepare your surface following the instructions in the preparation chapter, pages 162–63. The walls had a white base coat in place.

step 1 Draw a zigzag pattern on craft paper that will reach right across the wall, and cut it out.

step 2 **(Shot 1)** Secure the paper pattern to the wall with spray adhesive and low-tack tape. Tape the edges neatly so that they become part of the pattern.

step 3 **(Shot 2)** Mix the indigo blue glaze. Pour some into the paint tray and load the mop with the blue glaze as you would a paint roller. Apply the color as if you were washing the walls, producing light and dark areas and a cloudy effect. Let dry 2 to 4 hours.

step 4 **(Shot 3)** Remove the paper pattern and touch up any leak lines.

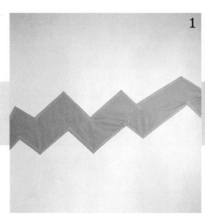
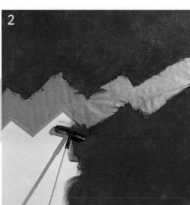
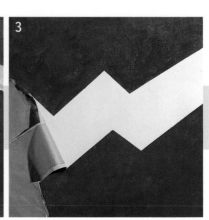

south seas wood
border molding

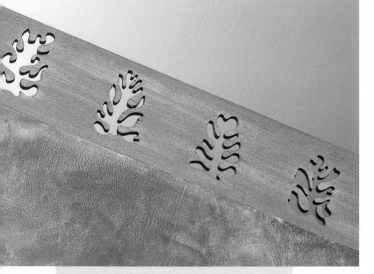

To make the bathroom wall less boxlike and to continue the South Seas theme, we added planks of wood and used a jigsaw to cut out seaweed shapes. The wood was distressed with paint to replicate driftwood.

MATERIALS AND TOOLS

½" or ⅝" MDF or wood plank

measuring tape

pencil

jigsaw

fine-grade sandpaper (optional)

peach brown and chocolate brown latex paint, satin

3" paintbrush

wire brush

step 1   Measure and cut the plank to the required length for your border molding. Draw the designs you have chosen onto the molding. (Make the patterns simple if you are not used to working with a jigsaw.)

step 2   **(Shot 1)** Cut out the pattern with the saw and sand smooth.

step 3   Apply the peach brown paint to the surface with the paintbrush. Let dry.

step 4   **(Shot 2)** Apply the chocolate brown paint over the surface, and before it dries rub across the surface with the wire brush in one direction to reveal the color underneath. Brush away more paint from around the cutout edges to accentuate their shape and to create the look of weathered driftwood.

tie-dyed curtains

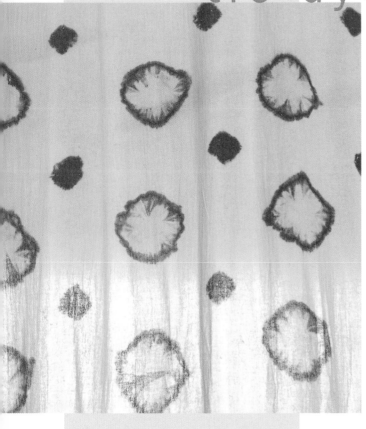

The technique of tie-dye has been used for thousands of years to add expression and pattern to cloth. Some of the tie-dye effects seen in African and Caribbean sarongs can be incredibly intricate and extremely beautiful, but they take many long hours to make. Simpler versions have been used by teenagers since the '60s and are once again popular not just for clothing but for bedding and curtains. If your fabric is colored rather than white, use a color remover in place of the dye to create patterns.

MATERIALS AND TOOLS

cotton fabric panel

fabric dye (we used Setasilk by Pebeo) or color remover (sold at drugstores and craft stores)

mixing container big enough to dip fabric into

marbles or golf balls

elastic bands

foam brush

step 1   **(Shot 1)** Prepare the dipping solution as instructed on the package.

step 2   **(Shot 2)** Tie off shapes using the marbles or the golf balls held tightly with elastic bands so that the dye won't penetrate the elastic bands.

step 3   Dip the tied-off balls into the dye until the material is saturated. Alternately, you can use a foam brush and paint the dye onto the fabric.

step 4   Remove the elastic bands and repeat the pattern in the next position.

Option: If your fabric is dark (colored), follow the same procedure, but dip into decolorant instead of dye.

To fix the color, put the curtains through a cold-water wash.

 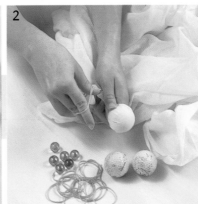 

Tuscany is a region of Italy with great charm and serenity. The Tuscan countryside possesses unimaginable beauty and also has a history bathed in great art and architecture. There are palaces, cathedrals, castles, and villas of the most extraordinary grandeur. No other place on earth is so concentrated in great art, yet it's the simple tones of the stone exteriors that best convey the spirit of this area. It's the way the light falls against an ancient wall, how colors are blended and softened with time; natural colors taken directly from the sun-bleached earth and the stone and marble floors used to cool their interiors. Whether an Italian home is a rural farmhouse or a villa perched on a hill, the living room is the most flexible room in the house, as Italians love to receive guests. These rooms evolve over the centuries with rustic furnishings alongside superb antiques, and they are always welcoming.

"I love Italy, especially Tuscany with its centuries-old villas and farmhouses. Today's modern materials make it easy to re-create the look of stone, plaster, and stucco, so you can relax into that old-world charm anywhere you choose."

This is one of four model rooms we decorated for a home show; the others are featured on pages 32, 54, and 84. To re-create my Tuscan fantasy, I transformed every surface into a stone facade. The upper walls have the silky smooth texture of Venetian plaster. Random patches of aqua, green, cream, and rose plaster were applied and then "buried" with a top coat of sand-colored plaster so that only hints of color showed through. Venetian plaster dries very hard, like marble, and because it has marble dust in it, you can burnish it with a spatula to achieve a polished sheen. For the lower wall, I stenciled realistic mosaic tiles with stucco that had been tinted the same accent colors as the upper wall. The concrete floor was brushed and rubbed with various stone shades to accentuate the crevices and build up color. And even the fireplace was re-created in the image of stone. A crown mantel was built to top the existing fireplace box, and the surround layered and decorated with molds, both stenciled and carved from stucco and cement. Wrought-iron accessories and grand but comfortable furnishings complete the Tuscan style.

tuscany

venetian plaster walls

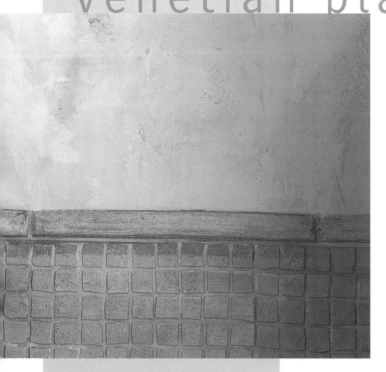

One of the most exciting materials for walls that has recently appeared on the market is Venetian plaster. Unlike traditional plaster, Venetian plaster is far superior in quality and effect. Pretint it and apply it in thin smears with a spatula. This plaster can be left flat or polished to a high, silky sheen, which is made possible by the marble dust that has been added to the plaster.

MATERIALS AND TOOLS

Venetian plaster

mixing containers

stir sticks

steel spatulas

rags

water

accent colors: green, aqua, cream, and rose tinted plaster

sand tinted plaster

Prepare your surface following the instructions in the preparation chapter, pages 162–63. Venetian plaster should be tinted with small amounts of universal tint mixed well. It will dry 50 percent lighter than it goes onto the wall.

step 1 **(Shot 1)** Apply streaks of each colored plaster randomly over the primed wall with a small spatula.

step 2 **(Shot 2)** Mix sand-colored tint into the container of Venetian plaster. Stir well. Apply a skim coat over the entire surface, covering the colored streaks, but leaving hints of color peeking through. Let dry 1 to 3 hours depending on the thickness of the plaster.

step 3 **(Shot 3)** Flatten the blade of the steel spatula against the wall and go over the surface, smoothing the peaks. The friction will polish the surface to a silky finish.

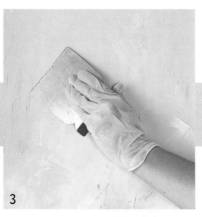

1   2   3

mosaic tiles

MATERIALS AND TOOLS

same as for Venetian Plaster Walls (see page 108)

Mylar or thick plastic sheets

marker and ruler

X-acto knife

spray adhesive

medium grade sandpaper (optional)

very fine sand (optional)

Stenciling with plaster is a fabulous alternative to stenciling with paint. The final image will be raised in relief rather than flat against the surface. You can use any type of plaster, but if the application is too thick it can crack eventually, once the plaster dries out. It is preferable to use Venetian plaster as it is less likely to crack and it takes pigment well. A simple stencil was made and the plaster pretinted and troweled over the top. When the stencil is removed, the surface has the look and feel of mosaic stone tiles.

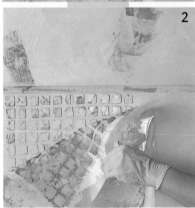

Prepare your surface following the instructions in the preparation chapter, pages 162–63.

step 1 Over a primed surface, apply a skim coat of sand-colored Venetian plaster (the top coat of the upper wall). This will show as the rough lines between the tiles.

step 2 Draw several stencils of approximately 1″ squares on Mylar; some should be irregular to look like old mosaic tiles. Cut them out. You will work more quickly with a few stencils, as they need to be cleaned after each application of plaster.

step 3 **(Shot 1)** Spray the back of 1 stencil and position it on the wall. Using the same accent colors as for the Venetian Plaster Walls, apply the colored plasters with a spatula over the stencil, varying the shades to create a mosaic pattern.

step 4 **(Shot 2)** Remove the stencil carefully to reveal a raised mosaic pattern. Let dry.

step 5 **(Shot 3).** Give the faux tiles a light sanding if you want them smoother.

Option: If you want a rougher-textured tile, add very fine sand to your Venetian plaster: 45% sand to 55% plaster.

painted concrete floor

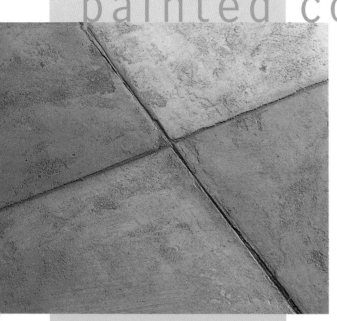

Colored concrete can look as interesting as stone. Paint can be used for an opaque finish, or thinned down and rubbed over a rough concrete surface to create the look of a stone floor. In the Tuscan living room on page 106, a fresh concrete floor was laid and while the concrete was still wet the edge of a spatula was dragged through it to imitate the look of separate stone slabs. If you are working on an existing concrete floor, use low-tack tape to mask off a stone grid, and then paint the stone slabs. Once dry, remove the tape and fill in the grout lines freehand using an artist's brush and burnt umber glaze. Seal the floor with several coats of varnish for protection.

MATERIALS AND TOOLS

¼" low-tack painter's tape (optional)

dusty rose, pale gray, blue gray, and beige latex paint, satin

sand-colored latex paint, satin

water-based glazing liquid

mixing containers

soft, clean, lint-free rags

burnt umber artist's acrylic paint

artist's brush

matte or satin acrylic varnish

foam brush or roller

RECIPE FOR STONE GLAZES

1 part latex paint

3 parts water-based glazing liquid

RECIPE FOR GROUT GLAZE

½ cup water-based glazing liquid

1 teaspoon burnt umber artist's acrylic paint

Prepare your surface following the instructions in the preparation chapter, pages 162–63. If your concrete floor doesn't have grooves to separate the stone slabs, mask off a grid using ¼" low-tack tape.

step 1 Mix the 4 accent colored glazes and the sand-colored glaze.

step 2 **(Shot 1)** Scrunch up a rag and dip it into one of the colored glazes. Rub the glaze over 1 concrete slab. Rub more off some areas. The color should vary a little as it would in real stone. Repeat for each stone slab, alternating colors to create a pattern you like. Let dry. Rub over the whole surface with the sand-colored glaze, muting the first colors.

step 3 **(Shot 2)** Mix the burnt umber glaze. If you have put the tape down, remove it. Fill in the grout lines freehand using an artist's brush and the burnt umber glaze.

step 4 Add 3 coats of varnish and let dry and cure for a few days.

The Punjab is a province in the north of India that is saturated in vibrant color. The fragrances and hues of the spice markets, crammed with over-full baskets of cinnamon, nutmeg, and saffron, play jubilantly against the jewel tones of Indian saris and the rich terra-cotta earth. This scorched landscape is the backdrop to the bright tones of daily life. We can learn so much from the way Indians use color—but why do these colors shock us back home. After battling your way home in rush hour traffic on a cold drizzly evening, how comforting it would be to be greeted by rooms filled with warm earth tones and splashes of the brightest lime, ruby red, and sapphire blue.

"I miss my country and I would like to give my home the flavor of India. I brought many things with me and want to know how to use them here."

Dipti emigrated from the north of India to Canada eight years ago. When I first met her she showed me boxes of the most wonderful artifacts that were tucked away because she did not feel they showed well in her North American home. Once we had explored her treasures, it was not difficult to get inspired to add color, pattern, and texture to Dipti's plain living room to create a fitting backdrop for her collections. The only architectural feature in the room was the fireplace, which we emphasized by applying a paprika-colored grass-weave effect to the surface and then hand-painting an Indian design that we pulled from one of Dipti's saris. A lighter tone of the spicy fireplace was washed over the walls, which added depth and color to an otherwise plain surface. Dipti had trunks full of saris in breathtaking colors ranging from deep emeralds to lemon yellows. Some were highly decorated but many were just long lengths of brightly colored sheers. I chose panels of orange and shocking pink and used ornate bangles to attach them to a curtain rod. In the evenings Dipti now returns to a sun-drenched home filled with happy memories of her homeland.

before

The living room was rather ordinary, but the fireplace was an interesting shape. The pale yellow walls did not represent the colors and textures the homeowner was accustomed to.

indian spice
living room

curry walls

MATERIALS AND TOOLS

butter and curry yellow latex paint,
    satin
roller and paint tray
water-based glazing liquid
mixing container
soft, clean, lint-free rags

RECIPE

1 part curry yellow latex paint
2 parts water-based glazing liquid

Deep yellow ocher would look heavy and somber on its own as an opaque layer of paint. Here we mixed the color with glazing liquid and washed the colored glaze over the surface. The glazing liquid makes the color translucent so that the yellow base coat is allowed to glow through, creating many different shades of ocher. The result is exotic and mysterious, a perfect backdrop for the flavors of India.

Prepare your surface following the instructions in the preparation chapter, pages 162–63.

step 1 Apply 2 coats of butter yellow base coat and let dry for 4 hours.

step 2 Mix the curry yellow glaze.

step 3 Scrunch up a rag and dip it into the colored glaze. Rub the color onto the walls, going back on your work and dabbing to get rid of any hard lines. This technique will produce lighter and darker areas of color that blend together gently.

sari curtains and tea box finial

Panels of Dipti's light and airy Indian fabrics were used to make curtains, and we found new life for some of her jewelry by using brightly colored bracelets as curtain rings. We made finials by painting tea boxes a pattern that complements the one bordering the fireplace. A visit to a sari store is like experiencing an Aladdin's cave of color. Trinkets abound, and saris are available in every possible color and price range.

fireplace and painted detail

The hand-painted border ensures that the fireplace is a major focal point in the living room. The design was traced from sari material and filled in with brilliant colors in keeping with the Indian theme.

MATERIALS AND TOOLS

orange terra-cotta latex paint, satin

water-based glazing liquid

mixing container

roller and paint tray

plastic stippling tool (also known as denim brush)

paper towels

design (we copied a design from a piece of Indian fabric)

cardboard for design template

pencil

sharp knife

low-tack painter's tape

artist's acrylic paints in vibrant colors

artist's brushes

gold paint pen

straight-edge ruler

mirrored Con-Tact paper

scissors

RECIPE

1 part orange latex paint

1 part water-based glazing liquid

Before we began this part of the project, the fireplace surround was colorwashed in the same manner as the Curry Walls, page 114.

step 1 **(Shot 1)** Mix the orange glaze and apply it over the colorwashed base of the fireplace surround.

step 2 **(Shot 2)** Using the stippling tool, scrape through the wet glaze in straight horizontal strokes. You will see some of the base coat coming through. Wipe the excess glaze off the stippling tool after each stroke. Then gently pull the stippling tool through the glaze from top to bottom so that lines will run in both directions. Let dry thoroughly.

step 3 **(Shot 3)** Draw a template of the design you have chosen onto a piece of cardboard and cut it out. Tape the template in position and trace the designs around the surround with pencil.

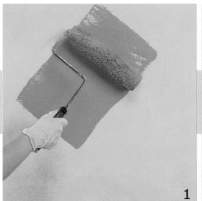

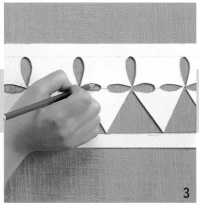

step 4 **(Shot 4)** Paint in the forms in a variety of colors using an artist's brush and artist's acrylics.

step 5 **(Shot 5)** Outline the forms with a gold paint pen, using a ruler for the straight lines.

step 6 **(Shot 6)** Cut out circles from the mirrored Con-Tact paper and stick them onto the design. Outline the circles with a contrasting artist's acrylic.

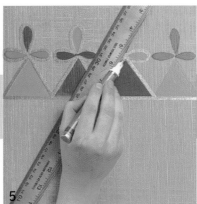
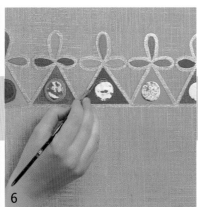

The Gothic style that swept through Europe and parts of America in the middle 1800s was whimsical and highly decorative, a revival of medieval design, but with more pomp and glory, a style that celebrated a period of huge prosperity for the rich landowners, governments, and industrial barons. It was an interpretation of the glorious colors and shapes that decorated the walls and carvings of Europe's medieval cathedrals and churches. Gothic architecture represented power and can be seen in Victorian public buildings, country estates, and city town houses all over the world. Although the buildings were often somber, with their arched windows and doors protected by ugly stone gargoyles, the interiors were lavish, with carved ceilings and marble paneled walls. Today we are seeing a boom in the economy, and luxurious materials and craftsmanship are once again popular in home decorating. Gold leafing, elaborate moldings, carved ceilings, and marble interiors are all available—for those who can afford them. But there are numerous tricks and products that will help you produce the illusion of opulence without the cost. There are moldings made from fiberglass, carved ceiling panels and tiles molded from plastic, and every type of floor that can be laid by the novice do-it-yourselfer. And, of course, paint—the best decorating tool there is. So, if you want to create your own Gothic style, it's all possible *and* affordable.

"We fell in love with this carved wood chandelier, bought it, and then found it was far too grand for our dining room"

Newlyweds Marco and Donna are in an exciting stage of married life. They are collecting furnishings and building a home for their future. Their taste runs to heavy wood furnishings, but the house has the clean aesthetic of today's architecture. They wanted a sumptuous dining room with a sense of grandeur. The ceiling was covered with a prepainted plastic tile, creating an amazing surface. With a ceiling this exotic, the walls had to compete. They were roughly textured in yellow ocher to give them an ancient, faded effect. I divided the walls with a wine-colored chair rail with an architectural stencil layered over the top. The dado was then richly painted with panels of different marbles. This room took several weekends to complete, but the deep colors, heavy marbles, and faded walls gave Marco and Donna their own Gothic castle.

before

Solid wood furniture inherited from Marco and Donna's Italian parents sat clumsily in this plain dining room.

gothic castle

gothic ceiling

Embellished ceilings have suddenly become fashionable again. Although I do prefer a plain white ceiling, today there are products available that will give you the grandeur of a bygone age. The oversized tiles we used here are designed to be painted and are produced in different patterns taken from original old European ceilings. It is much easier to paint and decorate the tiles before they are installed.

MATERIALS AND TOOLS

plastic ceiling tiles (see Resources)

high-adhesion primer

2" paintbrush

terra-cotta, burgundy, mustard yellow, and aqua latex paint, satin

water-based glazing liquid

mixing container

1" and 2" fitches or small paintbrushes

stippling tool or wide, flat-ended, stiff bristle paintbrush

3 ½" artist's brushes

bronze metallic paint

RECIPE

1 part burgundy latex paint

2 parts water-based glazing liquid

step 1 Use a primer designed to cover slippery surfaces to prime the tiles.

step 2 **(Shot 1)** Apply 2 coats of terra-cotta base coat with the paintbrush, making sure to get into all the pattern's crevices. Let dry.

step 3 **(Shot 2)** Mix the burgundy glaze. Apply the glaze to the tile and then stipple over the surface to give a mottled effect. Let dry.

step 4 **(Shots 3 and 4)** Use the mustard and aqua paints and artist's brushes to highlight some of the relief pattern details.

step 5 Paint over the colored details with a translucent coat of the bronze metallic paint.

1   2   3   4

aged walls

MATERIALS AND TOOLS

white and ocher latex paint, satin
roller and paint tray
water-based glazing liquid
mixing container
low-tack painter's tape
cheesecloth

RECIPE

1 part ocher latex paint
2 parts water-based glazing liquid

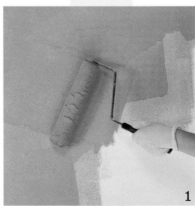

1

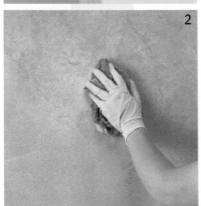

2

To give the illusion of old plaster walls that have texture and transparency, all you need is a colored glaze and a roll of cheesecloth. Use Mediterranean colors that have muted tones like ocher, dusky rose, and shades of pale terra-cotta.

Prepare your surface following the instructions in the preparation chapter, pages 162–63.

step 1   Apply 2 coats of white base coat and let dry for 4 hours.

step 2   **(Shot 1)** Mix the ocher glaze. Work on one wall at a time, masking off the other walls with low-tack tape so that you have neat corners. Roll on the glaze in 3′ or 4′ squares, working quickly so that you keep a wet edge and won't have lap lines (see page 159 in the preparation chapter).

step 3   **(Shot 2)** Dab the wet glaze with a handful of scrunched-up cheesecloth to get rid of obvious roller marks and give the surface some texture. Don't overdo it. This should be quick, simple, and very loose.

step 4   Roll glaze onto the next section, overlapping the wet edges and dabbing them first with the cheesecloth to prevent lap marks.

step 5   When you have finished one wall, let it dry completely for 4 hours or more, depending on the glazing liquid. Remove the tape and reposition over the finished edge to avoid paint buildup at the corners.

three-marble dado

MATERIALS AND TOOLS

white latex paint, satin

roller and paint tray

pencil and ruler

level

low-tack painter's tape

pale green, dark spruce green, tan, and
    rust latex paint, satin

water-based glazing liquid

mixing container

2 small foam rollers

cellophane wrap

black watercolor pencil

1½" foam brush

badger-hair or soft bristle paintbrush

acrylic spray varnish

semigloss acrylic varnish

foam brush

Man has been reproducing the look of marble with paint for centuries. It was ordinary people's way of having lavish marble detail in their homes, similar to the ones that could be seen in churches and cathedrals, without the cost. Today, we can add elegance and a sense of fun by using a combination of different stones. Here I used 3 different marbles as a dado, finished with an architectural stencil as a chair rail. The white background marble is a delicate finish with just a few veins. The diamonds are Rosso Verona marble, and Verde Antico marble is a heavy, rich effect that surrounds each panel. All these marbles are simple to do but create a complex and interesting detail on these dining room walls.

Prepare your surface following the instructions in the preparation chapter, pages 162–63.

step 1 Apply 2 coats of white base coat to the dado and let dry for 4 hours. Mark out the dado design you want. Here I did large panels, 3' high and 5' wide. I then divided each panel by masking off a box within a box and a diamond shape with low-tack tape. (Work on one marble at a time, and once you have completed one marble, let it dry and then retape so that the marbles meet each other.)

step 2 **(Shot 1)** For the outer band of Verde Antico, apply 2 coats of pale green base coat and let dry.

RECIPE FOR VERDE ANTICO GLAZE

1 part dark spruce green latex paint
2 parts water-based glazing liquid

RECIPE FOR ROSSO VERONA GLAZE

1 part rust latex paint
1 part water-based glazing liquid

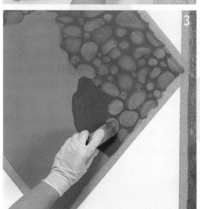

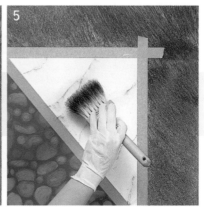

step 3 **(Shot 2)** Mix the dark spruce green glaze and roll it over the pale green base coat. Take a 12″ piece of cellophane wrap and fold it up into pleats. Press the pleated wrap diagonally onto the glaze, lift, and press down again, moving randomly over the band but always in the same diagonal direction. Don't press too hard or you will make impressions of your fingerprints. Let dry for about 4 hours, depending on glaze.

step 4 **(Shot 3)** Retape for the diamond. Fill in the diamond with 2 coats of tan base coat and let dry for 2 hours. Mix the Rosso Verona glaze. Work in very small areas: Roll on the glaze and then, using the end of a soft, dry foam roller, rub irregular oval and round shapes. Make them all different sizes. You don't need to take all of the glaze off. Leave a slight texture of color to add depth. Let dry.

step 5 **(Shot 4)** Retape for the remaining triangles. Apply a thin layer of water-based glazing liquid over a white triangle with the 1½″ foam brush. Using a wet black watercolor pencil, draw in thin, jagged veins on the diagonal.

step 6 **(Shot 5)** Soften the lines with the badger-hair brush. Let dry.

step 7 Apply 1 coat of spray varnish to seal. (The watercolor pencil veins will run if you brush varnish over them.) Then apply 2 coats of semigloss varnish with a foam brush to the other areas of the dado to add the depth and sheen of authentic marble.

country rooms

Country living and country decorating are a simpler way of life. Fashions change at a much slower pace, so there is no threat of your living or dining room furnishings becoming outdated in the next design wave. Decorative finishes have always been a part of the country style. Folk painting, stenciling, and colorwashing were ways to add spirit and design to houses that were often built on a less lavish scale than their wealthy city cousins, and they were less expensive than the wallpapers, fancy rugs, or fine wood furniture that adorned urban homes. These time-honored techniques have remained largely unchanged for hundreds of years. Fine wallpapers were rarely used in European cottages; instead, lime washes were rubbed over bare plaster walls, resulting in luminous and translucent finishes. Today, a less toxic alternative is colorwashing with water-based paints, which is a fast and inexpensive way to add depth and color to modern walls.

Over the last decade, I've noticed a new country style developing, one that is fresher and younger. Period styles like the Arts and Crafts Movement are still highly popular today, but instead of the original heavy wood paneling and dark somber colors, lighter tones are being employed. Inspiration is taken from the architecture of Greek Revival but used in interiors as a way of dressing up today's plainer structures. Light pastels, colorwashed over creamy whites, work just as well with country furnishings as the darker traditional country colors. Whichever palette you choose for a country living room or dining room you can be assured that this long-lasting, relaxing look will be enjoyed by everyone.

I always say that decorating is a state of mind. If you crave the simplicity of country furnishings but live your life in the center of a busy city, it's okay to break the rules. There's no reason not to create your own country haven in a third-floor walk-up. Urban country is about using lighter, fresher colors to open up and enhance a room. Colors are inspired by the surrounding seasons; that particular green when leaves first open, or a Granny Smith apple; a field of wheat, or the delicate whites of a bunch of daisies. Instead of using solid layers of paint, colorwashes are softly burnished over walls to make the light dance off their surfaces. Old farmhouse chairs sit comfortably alongside much-loved but mismatched pieces. The mood of Urban Country is a blend of city sophistication and relaxed country charm.

"My goal was to incorporate my beloved pine table

and chairs into my new city apartment."

When Dana, my wonderful assistant, moved into her new home in a downtown apartment building, she brought her much-loved painted pine chairs and farmhouse-style table with her. They had been antiqued and crackled in vintage greens and reds. Dana is a young woman living in the city, so the challenge was to incorporate her love of country furniture into an urban setting. Fresh apple green squares were painted on the walls, and since privacy was not an issue, the recessed window became the focal point. Instead of using curtains, I drew attention to the shape with ornate iron urns that were bought sliced in half so they fit flush against the wall. The finishing touch was two topiaries stylized for a city dwelling.

before

This is a 1920s city apartment with white walls and woodwork and a beautiful bay window.

urban country

simply squared walls

Here the walls were given a rustic flavor by our filling in the squares freehand instead of taping them off. We didn't want perfect squares but more of a floaty feeling.

MATERIALS AND TOOLS

white and pale green latex paint, satin
roller and paint tray
pencil and measuring tape
chalk line
level
water-based glazing liquid
mixing container
3" foam brush
soft, clean, lint-free rags

RECIPE

1 part pale green latex paint
3 parts water-based glazing liquid
1 part water

Prepare your surface following the instructions in the preparation chapter, pages 162–63.

step 1 Apply 2 coats of white base coat and let dry for 4 hours.

step 2 **(Shot 1)** Measure and mark 18″ intervals across and down each wall. Use a chalk line to mark out the grid. Check your lines with a level to make certain they are straight. Use a colored chalk similar to your intended paint color.

step 3 **(Shot 2)** Mix the pale green glaze. Apply the glaze to every other square with a foam brush, creating a checkerboard effect. Work on one square at a time.

step 4 **(Shot 3)** While the glaze is still wet, rub the square softly with a rag to create a slightly dragged and antiqued effect.

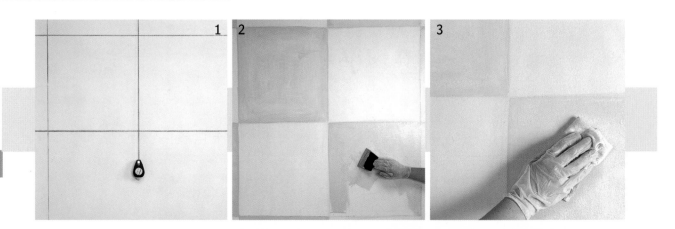

antiqued table

Although Dana bought the table in her dining room finished, a crackle medium can be applied to a new table to give it a rustic look. There are many ways to age a new surface, from layering on paint and then sanding back to wear down areas to applying a crackle medium that will make the new paint appear split and old. The best effect is when all of these are used together. You can't go wrong when you experiment with antiquing. If you make a mistake, then just sand down the section you don't like. The following instructions show how to create a central panel of crackle on the tabletop with an antiqued border.

MATERIALS AND TOOLS

dark brown latex paint, satin

brush or small roller and paint tray

low-tack painter's tape

crackle medium

2 foam brushes

burnt umber and wicker white artist's
acrylic paint

craft paper

2" natural bristle brush

pale gray latex paint, satin

3" paintbrush

rag

oil-based varnish, non-yellowing

yellow-brown artist's oil

toothbrush

FOR ADDED DECORATION
(OPTIONAL)

mango artist's acrylic paint (and other
colors of choice)

a small amount of water-based glazing
liquid

a plate

artist's brushes

RECIPE

½ cup oil-based varnish

½ teaspoon yellow-brown artist's oil

Antiqued Table Continued

Prepare surface according to the instructions in the preparation chapter, pages 162–63.

step 1 Apply 2 coats of dark brown base coat and let dry for 4 hours.

step 2 **(Shot 1)** In the center of the table, mark out and tape a large rectangle or panel using the low-tack painter's tape. Make sure to press the tape down securely to avoid leakage. Apply crackle medium to the center rectangle with a foam brush. Let dry (or follow the instructions on the bottle).

step 3 **(Shots 2 and 3)** Put a blob each of burnt umber and wicker white artist's acrylics beside each other on a piece of craft paper. Pull the 2" natural bristle brush through the 2 paints together to create streaks. Apply in long, single strokes over the crackle medium. Let dry for 4 hours.

step 4 **(Shot 4)** Reverse the tape in order to create texture around the outside of the rectangle. Dip a coarse 3" brush into pale gray paint, remove the excess onto a rag, and dry-brush over the surface, brushing in only one direction. Remove the tape.

step 5 **(Shot 5)** Prepare the tinted oil-based varnish according to the recipe, and brush some over the surface of the crackled panel. It's best to use oil-based varnish, as water-based could make the crackle medium react and mar the look that has already been created.

step 6 **(Shot 6)** Dip a toothbrush into the pale gray paint and splatter over the surface of the dragged area outside the rectangle.

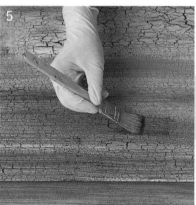

step 7   **(Shot 7)** Add decoration if you like. Here we separated the two parts with a freehand line. Put a blob of the mango acrylic paint and a blob of water-based glazing liquid on a plate. Pull an artist's brush through the paint first and then pick up a bit of glazing liquid. When you draw the line the color blurs slightly, creating a soft, blended accent.

step 8   Apply at least 3 coats of untinted oil-based varnish to the entire surface.

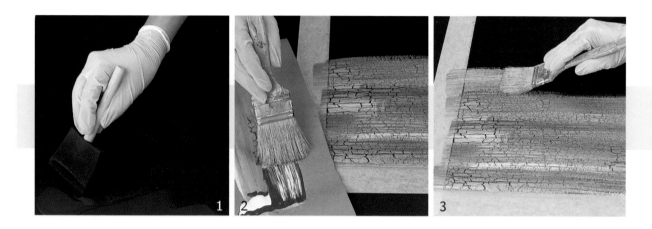

Greek Revival was the first American style to emerge after the United States became independent from Great Britain. The young democracy looked to the architecture of the first democratic country. Up until this period important buildings were designed around the Colonial style and featured wide edifices with a central door and windows spaced equally apart. The Greek Revival style copied ancient structures like the Parthenon on the Acropolis in Athens. Painted white pillars, columns, and stone were used instead of the traditional wood. Government buildings, town halls, and important structures up and down the East Coast began to resemble Greek temples. The power of this strong style of architecture can be incorporated into an interior room to give it strength and masculinity.

"I wanted a room that was masculine

but homey at the same time."

Randy, an airline pilot, spends a lot of time in impersonal hotel rooms, so when he finally returns from work he wants a real home, with an inviting living room. The uninspiring brick fireplace was the natural focal point of the room, but because Randy's apartment was a rental we were not allowed to touch it. I decided to build a facade over the existing structure, one that could be easily removed when he left the apartment. I built a box from MDF and slotted it over the brick facade. My inspiration for the shape of the new fireplace surround and the decoration around the window was taken from Greek Revival style. Rather than dressing the window with curtains or blinds, I used some decorative molding, motifs, and paint to build the theme. The fluted side columns are a clever but easy trompe l'oeil design. The metal door was finished in a faux wood, simply grained to replicate a deep mahogany.

Today's country colors are far more interesting for this room. The deep turquoise on the walls is not an obvious first choice, but it is a color that works equally well both with sophisticated furnishings and with the canvas slip-covered sofas and country pieces here.

This room has beautiful woodwork and trim but a rather ugly fireplace and dated furnishings.

before

greek revival

fireplace facade

I wanted to change the appearance of this unattractive fireplace so that it would blend in with the Greek Revival spirit of the room. Instead of painting the brick or covering it in plaster, I used sheets of MDF. I kept the original wood mantel and built the facade over the brick. You will need two pieces for the sides and one for the front of the fireplace. I added some molding for a little detail, then primed the structure and applied a golden yellow base coat. **(Shots 1 and 2)** To antique the wood, I wiped burnt umber water-based stain over the surface, leaving a buildup of stain behind in the corners and crevices around the molding.

window decoration

If privacy is not an issue, then windows can be given an architectural feature to dress them up. In keeping with the Greek Revival theme, I drew a temple shape around the windows and balcony door and masked it off. Once the base coat was on the wall, I was left with the white shape. The masking tape was reversed over the base coat and the shape painted with 2 coats of cream paint. This was rubbed over in the same way as the fireplace on page 135 to lightly texture the surface. A 5-point star was stenciled in the center using a two-step stencil. For added definition, strips of molding were nailed along the top of the window and then up to form a triangle. The molding was treated to the same faux wood effect as the door (see page 138). The columns on either side of the window were given an architectural feel with trompe l'oeil fluting.

fluted columns

Prepare your surface following the instructions in the preparation chapter, pages 162–63.

MATERIALS AND TOOLS

- pencil and ruler
- low-tack painter's tape
- light golden yellow latex paint, satin
- paintbrush
- a small amount of water-based glazing liquid
- white and pale orange artist's acrylic paints
- round-tip artist's brush
- dark gray pencil or pencil crayon
- burnt umber water-based stain
- soft, clean, lint-free rags
- acrylic varnish
- foam brush

step 1 Measure and mask off the columns with low-tack tape. Ours are 8″ wide. Apply 2 coats of light yellow base coat and let dry for 4 hours.

step 2 Measure and draw in the 3 flutes, rounding each end. Ours are ½″ wide with 2″ between each flute and 1¼″ at the edge of the column.

step 3 **(Shot 1)** In this example, the light source (window) is on the left of the column, so the light would shine onto the right side of the flute. Dip the artist's brush into a bit of glazing liquid and then white acrylic and paint a line up the right side of each flute.

step 4 **(Shot 2)** For the shadow line, dip an artist's brush into a bit of glazing liquid and then pale orange acrylic and paint a line up the left side of each flute. Let the two colors blend in the center to show a gradual movement from light to dark. Let dry.

step 5 **(Shot 3)** Redo the lines in gray pencil to create more dimension.

step 6 **(Shot 4)** To antique and soften the effect, rub over the entire surface with the same burnt umber stain used on the fireplace surround on page 135.

step 7 Apply 1 or 2 coats of acrylic varnish with a foam brush to protect your work.

faux wood door

MATERIALS AND TOOLS

dark chicory brown latex paint, satin

paintbrush or roller and paint tray

yellow brown, red brown, and 2 mid-brown latex paints, satin

water-based glazing liquid

mixing containers

low-tack painter's tape

1″ paintbrushes

badger-hair or soft bristle paintbrush

flogger or long bristle paintbrush

satin acrylic varnish

burnt umber pigment (liquid or powder)

face mask if using powder

foam brush

RECIPE

1 part latex paint

1 part water-based glazing liquid

There are many techniques for replicating the look of real wood. The colors, grains, and knots differ with each type of wood, so it's a good idea to study the real thing to help you visualize the final outcome. Here I combined and blended 4 shades of brown to create the depth of mahogany. While the glazes were still wet, I used a flogger to make the grain lines. The outcome is quite authentic, and far more interesting than a plain metal door.

Prepare your surface following the instructions in the preparation chapter, pages 162–63. This is a metal door, so it required a high-adhesion metal primer.

step 1   Apply 2 coats of chicory brown base coat and let dry for 4 hours. Mix the 4 faux wood glazes. With low-tack tape, mask off the door into sections that would be separate strips or panels of wood on a real wood door and paint each separately.

step 2   **(Shot 1)** With a 1" paintbrush, dab the yellow brown glaze over the surface in random patches. Always brush in one direction.

step 3   **(Shot 2)** Fill in some of the empty spots with the red brown glaze and continue with the lighter of the 2 mid-browns. Finish by closing up any holes with the darker mid-brown.

step 4   **(Shot 3)** Use the soft brush to blend the colors together by going over the surface lightly in one direction only, up and down and on a very slight diagonal.

step 5   **(Shot 4)** Using the flogger, slap the bristles against the surface, moving downward as you hit, to break up the glaze slightly and create a faux wood grain.

step 6   Tint the acrylic varnish with a bit of burnt umber and apply 2 to 3 coats with a foam brush for protection.

Note: Always wear a mask when mixing with a powder.

The Arts and Crafts movement took place near the end of the nineteenth century in England. It was a rebellion against the mass production of factory goods during the Victorian era. One of the great pioneers of that time was William Morris, who believed that interior design should be accessible to everybody, not just the rich. His passions ran from designing furniture and glass to textiles and wallpaper. William Morris's work is as popular today as it was at the turn of the twentieth century. His inspiring use of color and patterns taken from nature is still readily available in wallpapers and fabrics.

"I wanted to bring back my Arts and Crafts—style

living room to its former glory."

When Joyce and Victor asked me to help restore their dining room with a style that would complement the dark wood moldings and trim and the Victorian-style furnishings, I was immediately inspired by the designs and colors of the great William Morris. The room had high ceilings, gorgeous woodwork, and a plate rail, which are typically found in homes built around the turn of the last century. The original homeowners would probably have decorated this room with somber Victorian colors and possibly wood paneling. I decided to put back the look of paneling but with a lighter, fresher style more appropriate for today's decor, using paint instead of wood. Above the plate rail, Anaglypta, an embossed wallpaper that is designed to be painted, was applied and rubbed in tones of green to highlight the pattern. All the colors were lifted from the William Morris fabric used in the curtains—a pattern he designed more than one hundred years ago that can still be found in homes all over the world. Although I replaced the Tiffany light with an alabaster Arts and Crafts—style chandelier, the rest of Joyce's dark Victorian furnishings are now at home in the new dining room.

Powder blue swags and floral wallpaper did nothing to enhance the bones of this dining room.

before

arts&crafts

faux wall panels

MATERIALS AND TOOLS

pale yellow, white, and medium yellow
   latex paint, satin

roller and paint tray

pencil and ruler

level

low-tack painter's tape

1″ paintbrush

light and dark orange pencil crayons

Painted panels are a great way to add interest to walls. Here we used long panels topped by smaller ones. The size of the panels should be in proportion to the room. Use a level to make sure the panels are straight. The trick to making the panels look recessed is using tones of the same color. The mid tone is the base coat, the slightly darker tone is for the shadow lines; and the lightest is the highlight. All the measuring and taping takes a little patience, but the painting goes very quickly, and the results are worth it.

   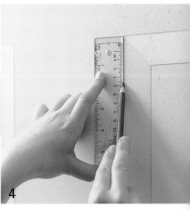

1 2 3 4

Prepare your surface following the instructions in the preparation chapter, pages 162–63.

step 1 Apply 2 coats of pale yellow base coat and let dry for 4 hours.

step 2 **(Shot 1)** Measure and mark off the panels; use a level to make sure they are straight. Then mask them off using low-tack tape. Here the outer perimeter of the small upper panels is 16″ wide by 15″ long, and it is 16″ wide by 36″ long for the lower panels. Tape again 1½″ inside the outer perimeters to create a border frame.

step 3 **(Shot 2)** Place low-tack tape horizontally across the top left and bottom right corners of each border frame. With the 1″ paintbrush and white paint, fill in the top and right-hand border. Let dry.

step 4 **(Shot 3)** Remove and replace the horizontal tape at the corners so that the white is covered. Now fill in the left-hand and bottom border with the medium yellow paint.

step 5 **(Shot 4)** Outline the painted borders using a ruler and the pencil crayons: light on outside, dark on inside. This will add more definition to the panels.

anaglypta border

MATERIALS AND TOOLS

Anaglypta border

heavy-duty vinyl adhesive

wallpaper paste brush

level

soft paintbrush

water-based primer

*soft yellow and avocado green latex
   paint, satin*

roller and paint tray

kitchen sponge

paper towels

rusty red artist's acrylic paint

artist's brush

Anaglypta is a heavy, embossed wallpaper that is designed to be painted. I chose this pattern because it was designed in a fashion similar to William Morris's papers. It is a ceiling pattern, which means the design runs vertically as well as horizontally. Because it was glued down horizontally, only a couple of rolls were required for the border. After the base coat was on, I gently smoothed paint over the surface with a kitchen sponge, highlighting the embossed pattern. For the finishing touch, I hand-painted in a small part of the detail.

Prepare your surface following the instructions in the preparation chapter, pages 162–63.

step 1 To apply the Anaglypta wallpaper border: Unroll the paper and cut it along the perforations. Apply vinyl adhesive to the back of the paper with a brush, including all the embossed valleys and indentations. Apply the adhesive to the wall as well. Wait 10 minutes for the paper to absorb the glue—the paper will stretch a bit. Place the paper on the wall, using a level to ensure it's straight. Any gaps between the paper and the ceiling trim can be filled in later with spackle. Press the paper to the wall with your fingertips, then a brush. As the paper dries, the relief work will return to its original height. Let it dry completely. Prime with water-based primer.

step 2 Apply 2 coats of the soft yellow base coat to the Anaglypta with a roller and let dry for 4 hours.

step 3 **(Shot 1)** Dip a moist kitchen sponge into the avocado green paint. Remove the excess onto a paper towel. Softly sweep across the embossed surface to highlight the design. Don't press too hard or use too much paint.

step 4 **(Shot 2)** Color in some of the embossed details with the rusty red artist's acrylic and an artist's brush.

Italy is a feast for the eyes. For centuries Mediterranean people have been decorating their homes inside and out using ingenious techniques with a paintbrush. The walls of whole villages are decorated with the most marvelous murals and trompe l'oeils. Italians are also experts at blending the old with the new. An ugly concrete building in the center of a medieval town will be given a face-lift to blend in with its ancient neighbors, or a home with cracked plaster walls will be decorated with postmodern furnishings. Stone, marble, and granite have long been standard materials in most homes, not only those of the wealthy, as they are an excellent means to cool interiors in the sizzling summers. Marble is, of course, expensive and impossible to lay in areas such as ceilings. To solve this problem, artisans have been replicating the intricacies of numerous stones since the days of Pompeii.

It is the magnificent light that makes these homes even more special. Whereas heavy curtains are traditionally hung in northern European homes to keep out the cold, wooden shutters appear in southern regions to diffuse the sunlight.

"We designed and built our country house

and wanted something different from

the traditional country decor."

The owners of this newly built country house had just moved in, and although they knew their living room had great potential, they were at a loss as to where to begin. I took my inspiration from Italian villas with their spartan furniture and walls veiled in luminous color, awash in sunlight. Once the homeowners agreed to replace their leather furniture with an Italian sofa, I could then begin to coordinate the walls. A veiling technique was brushed over the upper part, and a low dado was painted in delicate marble panels. A palette of peaches and dove grays was chosen, and a weightier gray stone effect was applied to the fireplace to anchor the room. All the sheers and heavy curtains were removed and replaced with white wooden shutters. The delighted homeowners now have their own country villa.

The room had good bones and a well-proportioned fireplace, but the existing decor was bland and unimaginative.

country villa

veiling

Veiling is a gentle paint finish. Whispers of paint are washed over walls to create thin, translucent layers. The paint must be diluted with glazing liquid to create this effect. Two or even 3 different colors can be used, but experiment first on a small section of the wall or on a board.

MATERIALS AND TOOLS

light peach, white, and dark peach latex paint, satin

low-tack painter's tape

water-based glazing liquid

mixing containers

wide natural bristle brush

soft, clean, lint-free rags

badger-hair or soft bristle brush (optional)

RECIPE

1 part latex paint

2 to 3 parts water-based glazing liquid

Prepare your surface following the instructions in the preparation chapter, pages 162–63.

step 1 Apply 2 coats of the light peach base coat and let dry for 4 hours.

step 2 Work on one wall at a time and tape off the adjacent walls to make neat corners. When creating this effect, work in an area of 3' or 4', and keep a wet edge by moving quickly and applying the next section of color while the first is still wet to avoid lap lines.

step 3 **(Shot 1)** Mix the white and dark peach glazes. Brush the white glaze over the surface in diagonal waves, leaving darker and lighter areas.

step 4 **(Shot 2)** Immediately follow with the dark peach glaze, brushing it onto the lighter white areas.

step 5 **(Shot 3)** Lightly blend the colors together with a softening brush or a rag if necessary to create the feeling of transparent layers of color.

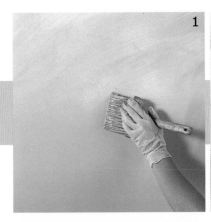
1

2

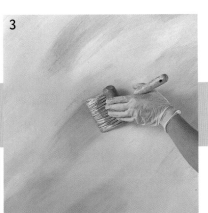
3

fantasy marble dado

This marble-panel dado anchors the room, and the delicate soft gray and beige tones coordinate beautifully with the peach veiling above. Flickers of gray veins over a white background give the illusion of marble. Simple lines of paint, an Italian technique for highlighting an area, are used to create the panels.

MATERIALS AND TOOLS

low-tack painter's tape

white, gray, yellow beige, and brown beige latex paint, satin

pencil and ruler

level

roller and paint tray

water-based glazing liquid

mixing containers

1" foam brush

badger-hair or soft bristle brush

cardboard

X-acto knife

spray adhesive

artist's brush

RECIPE

1 part latex paint

3 parts water-based glazing liquid

Prepare your surface following the instructions in the preparation chapter, pages 162–63.

step 1 Tape off an area approximately 3' high that is going to be the dado, and roll on 2 coats of white base coat. Let dry for 4 hours.

step 2 Draw and tape off the dado in approximately 3' by 5' panels. Use a level to make sure the panels are straight. Mix the gray and two beige glazes.

step 3 **(Shot 1)** Dip the foam brush into the gray glaze. Using the tip of the brush, paint in diagonal veins. They should move in the same direction, break off, and start up again further along the panel.

step 4 **(Shot 2)** Apply the darker beige glaze in areas around the gray veins.

step 5 **(Shot 3)** Fill in any openings in the panel with the yellow beige glaze.

(continued next page)

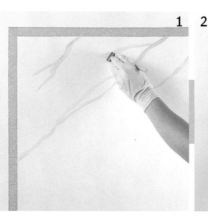

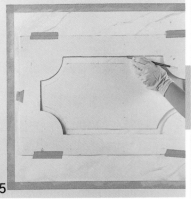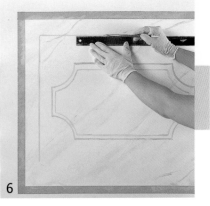

step 6 **(Shot 4)** With the softening brush held at right angles to the surface, soften and blend any harsh lines. Let dry completely.

step 7 **(Shot 5)** Cut out a cardboard template that represents the inset panels for the center of each large panel. Hold in position with tape. Using an artist's brush and the gray paint (without glazing liquid), draw in lines around the inset panels.

step 8 **(Shot 6)** Remove the template. Use a ruler and an artist's brush and gray paint to draw the outer lines.

faux stone fireplace

A plain white fireplace was given a sense of importance in this room. Because the walls are so soft and delicate, the fireplace needed to have strength. A simple stone finish was stippled over the surface in an earthy brown.

MATERIALS AND TOOLS

*rust brown, pale gray, and beige latex
 paint, satin*

water-based glazing liquid

mixing containers

cellulose kitchen sponge

*stippling brush or flat-topped hard bris-
 tle brush*

matte or satin acrylic varnish

foam brush

RECIPE

1 part latex paint

1 part water-based glazing liquid

Prepare your surface following the instructions in the
preparation chapter, pages 162–63.

step 1 Apply 2 coats of rust brown base coat to the fireplace surround and mantel and let dry for 4 hours.

step 2 **(Shot 1)** Mix the gray and beige glazes. Sponge the gray
glaze onto the surface, covering the area completely.

step 3 **(Shot 2)** Repeat immediately with the beige glaze.

step 4 **(Shot 3)** While the glazes are still wet, stipple the surface
and blend the 2 colors to remove any sponge marks. Leave a
hint of the rust base coat showing. Let dry.

step 5 Apply 2 or 3 coats of matte or satin varnish with a foam
brush.

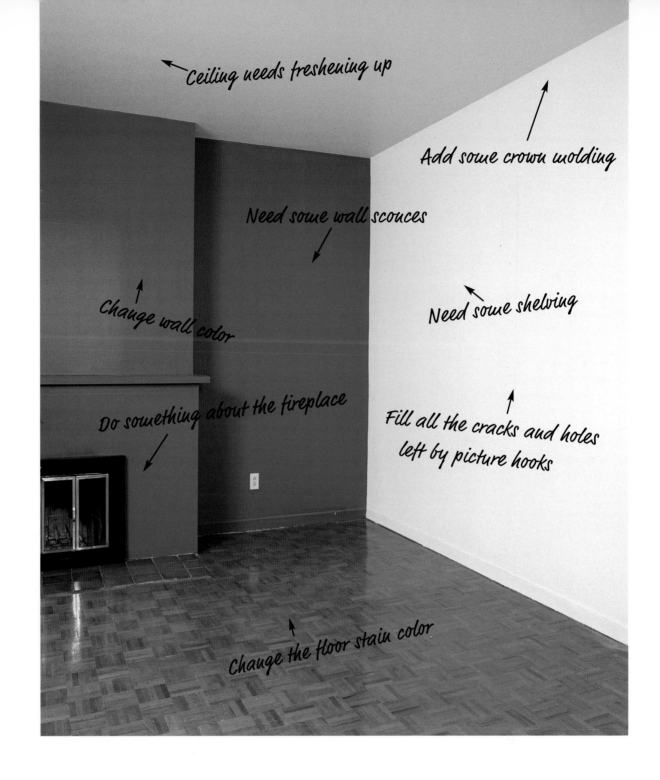

getting
prepared

set yourself up for success

Like you, we at The Painted House get many of our decorating ideas and inspiration from thumbing through glossy interior design books and magazines and watching television shows. The beautiful styling, innovative colors, and clever designs are seductive. But what's rarely seen or discussed is the time, planning, and number of talented people it takes to create these rooms. This does not mean that you cannot attempt your own room designs; however, in order to avoid frustration you must plan the project well. A successful room is as much about the planning as it is about your choice of colors.

If you organize the project well and pace yourself, the experience will be fun, and you'll still be in the mood to tackle other rooms in the home. Ask yourself how much time you have, and don't put an unrealistic time limit on the process. Surprises and delays are almost inevitable, so give yourself some leeway. Are there other people in the house to consider? Whether or not you're hoping for some help, check that it's a good time for them. The week before your child's exams or the year-end business meetings is not the time to disrupt the household order. Can you use another room to replace the one you are working in for the duration of the remodeling period? This consideration isn't as critical for a living or dining room as it is for a kitchen or bathroom, but you still need to address it.

The first step is to make a list of the preparations required to get your room ready for painting. Allocate the time needed depending on the size of the project. Are you having walls removed, electrical outlets changed or updated, or just adding extra molding or filling in a few cracks? Although thorough preparation of the walls, floors, woodwork, and trim is the least favorite job when you take on a decorating project, it separates a well-finished room from a mediocre one, and your work will last.

clean the room

Remove as much furniture as possible from the room and cover the remaining with sheets of plastic and then large drop cloths. On the floor, use heavy-duty drop cloths instead of plastic, which is extremely slippery. If you are removing carpet, now is the time to pull it out and take up any floor nails. Any wallpaper should be removed using either wallpaper remover gels or a commercial steamer. You can also carefully gouge the surface of the paper with the edge of a spatula—you don't want to scar the wall underneath, just make random rips. Then soak the walls with a wet sponge and start scraping. A combination of these methods works best for stubborn jobs.

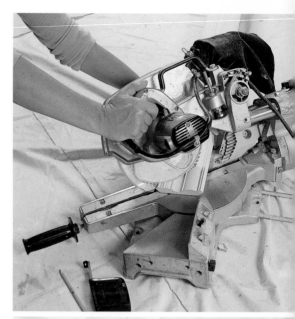

Invest in a good ladder. It will make the entire preparation and painting job much easier and safer. Wipe away any dust or cobwebs and wash the walls down with either trisodium phosphate (TSP) or vinegar and water to remove any surface grease or wallpaper residue.

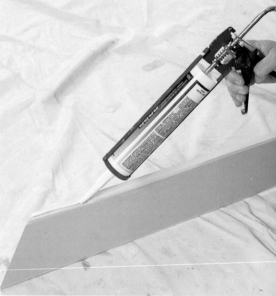

architectural details

Now is the time to remove any unwanted molding or trim, or to add some to the walls. You can buy stock molding in a variety of sizes and designs from lumberyards and hardware stores. It's available in wood, MDF, foam, and the more expensive plaster or custom-made, quality wood. Stock molding is relatively inexpensive and usually comes in 8-foot lengths. The width of the molding should be in proportion to the height of the ceiling. The higher the walls, the wider the molding. For the majority of 9-foot walls, 4- to 6-inch-wide moldings are adequate.

Crown molding is applied around the ceiling, baseboards on the wall at floor level, and trim around windows and doors. The standard molding from a hardware store is designed to be painted, and better-quality wood

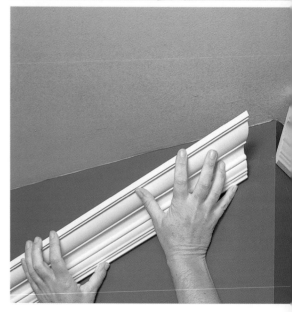

can be used for staining so that the grain of the wood can be seen.

Measure and cut the molding to size, using a miter box and saw for the edges. It is easier for two people working together to attach the molding. First use wood glue and then secure the piece in place with nails.

measuring and mitering

There are two types of miter cuts you will need for fitting the moldings together neatly around the walls: inside and outside corner cuts.

For an inside corner, the back of the molding is longer than the front. Measure from corner to corner on the wall, and mark that measurement on the back of the molding. Be sure the molding goes into the miter box so that the 45-degree cut angles in toward the front.

For an outside corner, the front of the molding is longer than the back. Measure from corner to corner on the wall and mark that measurement on the front of the molding. Place the molding into the miter box so that the cut angles in toward the back.

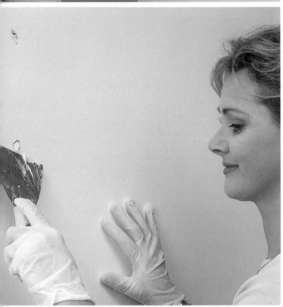

filling and repairs

It is important to fill cracks and holes and, if needed, to finish off the edge of any attached molding and trim with filler. To repair large cracks or holes, first brush away any loose plaster and debris and then fill. If the hole is deep, it is better to fill in thin layers, allowing each layer to dry before adding the next until you are flush to the wall. This will make a sturdier, shrink-resistant mending job. Ready-mixed filler is the easiest to use. You will need a scraper, fine-grade sandpaper, and a rag. Once all the plastered areas are dry, lightly sand over the surface to make sure the area is smooth.

the prime coat

Priming a surface serves several important purposes. The prime coat goes on after the surface has been cleaned and sanded and before the base coat is applied. Good-quality primers seal the surface and give it the tooth for paint to adhere. If you omit this step, you will need more coats of paint, and the paint job may look uneven; it will cost more time and money in the long run.

priming over plaster

Fresh plaster is very porous. It is imperative to apply a coat of primer to seal before painting. Always wait for at least a week for a freshly plastered wall to dry thoroughly before you prime. The plaster used for repairing cracks and holes dries much faster, and it also must be primed. Otherwise these spots will show through the fresh coat of paint.

priming over walls

There is no need to prime if you plan to paint a color over walls that have previously been coated in a light shade, and are clean and in good condition. If you are changing the color from dark to light, a prime coat will ensure that you get good coverage without having to apply many layers of paint.

There are stain-blocking primers that cover up nicotine, heat, watermarks, children's crayon, and other indelible marks. They ensure that these stains do not show through the fresh base coat.

Walls covered in wood paneling or wood veneer that is awkward to remove can be painted over to create a fresh new look. The wood paneling must first be sealed with wood primer to halt any knots, stain, or old varnish from coming through the new top coat. A light

sanding is required to buff up the surface and then a high-adhesion primer should be used.

If you have wallpaper on your walls and do not want to remove it, you can paint over the top of most papers as long as the paper is not peeling anywhere. Always test a small area first before applying the primer. It is possible that bubbling may occur due to absorption of water from the paint, but this usually disappears once the paper dries and shrinks back in place.

Painted woodwork that has been sanded down should be primed to seal any old paint or bare wood.

Any moldings and trim should be primed if they have been filled with plaster or they are new. Some trim is sold preprimed.

If you believe that your existing wall finish or trim is oil-based and you would like to work in water-based paint, then the oil surface must be sealed with a good-quality, high-adhesion primer. Latex (water-based) paint will not adhere to an oil-based surface. You can apply oil-based products over water-based paint without priming first.

working on ceilings

Prepare ceilings the same way you do walls: clean, fill any cracks, and prime darkly colored ceilings or fresh plasterwork. Paint the ceiling before the walls, and after all the preparation of the room is finished.

Most ceilings look their best painted white, as this opens up the room and reflects the color of the walls. A dark ceiling will make a room feel boxy unless you have very high ceilings. If you would like a color on the ceiling, use a low-luster latex paint.

Ceiling paint is a flat or matte white. It has a chalky texture and should never be used on walls. It is less expensive than regular paint but is not meant to be as durable and is impossible to clean.

The stucco ceilings common to new buildings must be primed with an oil-based primer. A water-based primer will soak into the pointy bits and they'll pull away from the ceiling, making quite a mess. You can apply water-based paint over an oil-based *primer*. (This is the one time the water-over-oil rule does not apply.)

Note: Always wear eye protection when you are working on the ceiling.

the base coat

Once all the plastering and priming is complete you are ready to apply the base coat. The base coat is applied either as the finishing color for the room or as the base color for a paint effect to be applied over the top.

Choose any sheen you prefer, but remember that the glossier the surface the more imperfections will show, and the flatter the surface the harder the paint is to clean and the more marks will show. A satin or velvet finish (depending on the manufacturer) is a good compromise.

If baseboards and trim are a feature, they look better highlighted with a semigloss finish. If they are inconsequential, blend them into the walls with a satin finish.

masking off

Always use low-tack painter's tape when you are masking off areas you don't want painted. Never underestimate the power of regular masking tape. It will pull off the primer, bits of plaster, and even varnish from the floor when you remove it.

First mask off the wall area to be painted. Mask around the ceiling molding, baseboards, and trim. If you have a stucco ceiling with no moldings it can be difficult to get a neat edge. A trick is to mask half an inch down from the ceiling so that the white of the ceiling goes onto the wall and your color on the wall is completely straight.

cutting in and applying paint

Once you've chosen the base color you will need a cutting-in brush. The best kind have angled bristles that help you paint a clean edge. You will also require a good-quality nap roller, paint tray, liners, and an extension pole.

Paint along the ceiling, trim, and baseboards with the cutting-in brush. Don't overload your brush. Dip only the first 2 inches of your brush into the paint, and apply in even strokes to the surface. Two thin coats are better than one thick coat.

Fill in the rest of the wall using the roller. To create a smooth finish, roll the paint on in a **W** shape until you have covered the wall in one even thin coat

Two coats of paint are usually required for the best coverage and durability. Water-based paint dries quickly to the touch, but let dry for 4 hours if painting another color or paint finish over the top, or if you'll be using tape. Oil-based paint requires twelve hours to dry.

painting woodwork and trim

Mask off the newly painted dry walls using low-tack painter's tape. Use a paintbrush or foam brush. Always apply the paint in the direction of the grain. If there is no grain, move along the length of the trim. Two coats are recommended.

keeping a wet edge

Keeping a wet edge is an expression you will see quite often in painting instructions for faux finishes. When you are applying a paint effect that requires blending different colors or creating patterns in the paint with rags or other tools, the paint must stay wet long enough to be manipulated. Because latex paint dries very quickly, you should apply water-based glazing liquid, which slows down the drying time, but does not change the color of your paint, giving you more time to work.

When applying a paint effect, it is necessary to work in manageable patches, 3 or 4 square feet at a time. As you move along, the edges of the patches must remain wet so that as you overlap the paint or glaze for the next section, it can be manipulated in the same way. If the edges have dried, you will get lap marks or lines around the patches and the effect will be ruined.

Work on one wall at a time and tape off the adjoining walls so that you won't get paint buildup in the corners. Begin at the top of the wall and work down to the bottom, then return to the top and keep going until you have finished the wall. Apply glaze to the first patch, work the effect (here we are ragging off), and then apply glaze to the next section, overlapping the edge slightly to ensure that it is wet. Work the effect starting at the edge and complete that patch. Continue in this manner until the wall is complete. If you find an edge has dried by the time you return to it, apply more glaze to open it up again, but it is important to work quickly. The best method is to work with a partner: one person applies the glaze and the other works the effect.

the floor

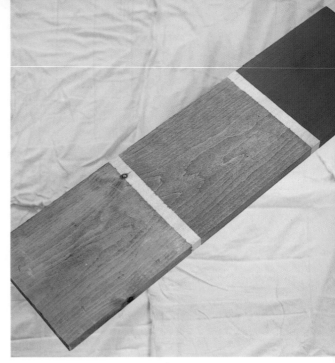

This sample board shows the result, left to right, of stain, paint wash, and pure paint on wood.

To strip, stain, and varnish a floor takes approximately five days. Make sure you don't need to use the room during this period and that you walk on it in only stocking feet for another week while the varnish cures and hardens.

Floors can be prepared at either the beginning or the end of the room makeover. Both times have advantages and disadvantages. If you have a lot of prep work and painting that will call for movement of ladders, I recommend doing the floor at the end to avoid scratching it; however, you will have to do some touch-ups on the freshly painted baseboards.

refinishing a wood floor

The first step is to sand down the surface using an industrial sander—a job best left to a professional. You can rent these sanders, however, and if you choose to do it yourself, take care not to gouge the wood. Remove 100% of the old varnish and stain so that you are left with the raw hardwood, parquet, and so on.

Wash the floor down and remove the dust from the walls. Let the room settle overnight and clean the floor again.

You are now ready to paint or stain the floor. Be careful not to spill any stain on areas that you do not plan to stain or you will have to resand.

decorating options for wood floors

wood stain

Wear gloves when working with stain. Soak a smooth rag in the stain and rub the stain over the wood in the direction of the grain, wiping off the excess to keep an even depth. Large areas can be applied with a kitchen mop, and the edges with a brush. The stain can be reapplied once the first coat has dried. The more coats, the more opaque the color will be.

You may choose two colors of wood stain and apply one as a border. Use masking tape pressed down firmly to separate the colors. To prevent bleeding, you may score the wood planks with a sharp knife, but this does leave a

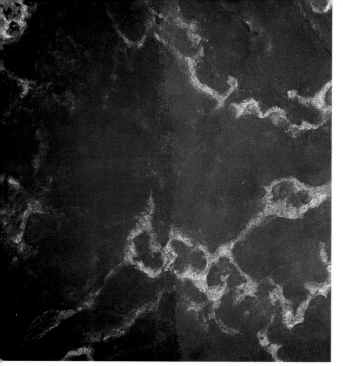

permanent scar in the wood's surface. Stain is permanent because it sinks into the wood, so it is important to check the colors first. To see the depth of the stain required, always test it in a corner and let dry.

paint wash

Watered-down latex paint can be applied like stain to create a colorwashed finish. This will create a pickled or driftwood effect, as if the wood has bleached and faded over time. Apply as you would stain.

One-half of this faux-marble board has a high-gloss varnish top coat, an important step to give the finish depth and authenticity.

pure paint

Paint sits on top of the wood fibers instead of sinking into the grain, so you will get opaque coverage, hiding any knots or natural wood shading. This is a good choice if the wood is marked or of a poorer grade. Paint is a great solution for plywood floors. To paint the floor, prime the wood first. If there are any knots, apply a special primer designed to seal them; a coat of shellac will seal them as well. Then apply 2 coats of water-based paint.

Freehand designs and stencils can be applied over stained or painted floors.

the top coat

The finishing touch for your floor is to apply four coats of varnish for protection and sheen. I adore a high-gloss sheen on floors, which is classic and elegant. But for a country-style floor, a low-luster sheen is more compatible. Certain paint effects call for a specific sheen to make them look authentic. Marble requires a high sheen to bring out its depth and pattern. Aged floors and painted details such as stenciling suit a flat finish.

Let each coat of varnish dry before applying the next. Water-based varnish will yellow less than oil-based, and good-quality water-based varnish is just as durable. To reduce stroke marks and give a smooth finish, use a varnish brush or a foam brush to apply the varnish.

Allow the floor to dry and cure for a few days before moving the furniture back into the room.

preparing surfaces for paint

surface	cleaning	repairs	sanding	sealer / prime coat
new drywall	Dust.	Add a skim coat of plaster if you want a very smooth finish.	Sand taped and plastered seams smooth.	If the drywall is not treated, prime it with water-based primer.
plaster walls (fresh or unsealed)	Use a damp sponge to clean. Let dry thoroughly.	Repair and fill holes with spackle.	Sand and dust gently, being careful not to scratch the surface.	All plaster must be sealed even if you are keeping it white. One coat of primer will seal the surface.
plaster or drywall previously painted	Sand off any loose paint. Wash with a damp sponge and let dry.	Repair nail holes and cracks with spackle.	If previous finish was glossy, sand lightly to rough up surface.	Prime with water-based primer.
stucco ceilings	Clean with a soft brush.	Fill cracks with spackle.	Sanding is not required as surface is rough.	Use stain-blocking primer if there is smoke or water damage. An oil-based primer is advisable to seal pointy stucco.
wood veneer walls or panels	Dust and wipe clean with damp rag. Let dry.	Repair holes with wood filler.	Sand lightly.	Prime with water-based or oil-based primer.
paper veneer wall panels	Dust and wipe clean with damp rag. Let dry.	Repair holes with wood filler or spackle.	Don't sand, as it will scar or remove the paper. Do sand the repaired spots.	Prime with oil-based primer, as water-based primer will soak in and loosen the paper.
new wood floors to stain	Dust and wipe clean with a barely damp rag. Too much water will raise the grain and could cause wood to warp. Allow to dry thoroughly.	Fill in any nicks and nail and screw holes with wood filler. It will take stain.	Sand any very rough spots first with heavy-grade sandpaper, then complete the piece with medium- or fine-grade paper. Always work in the direction of the grain. Remove dust with a damp rag, vacuum, tack cloth.	Seal any knotholes with shellac.
new wood floors to paint	Clean as for new wood floors to stain.	Fill in nicks and nail and screw holes with wood filler.	Sand as for new wood floors to stain.	Seal with shellac or a wood primer. Don't use water-based primer, as it will raise the grain. Oil-based primer requires only one coat, and you can paint over it with water-based paint.

surface	cleaning	repairs	sanding	sealer / prime coat
previously finished wood (painted, stained, or varnished)	Scrape away any loose dirt, peeling paint, or varnish with a bristle brush.	Repair any cracks or holes with wood filler.	If you are sanding the floor down to raw wood, use a commercial sander. Clean with soap and warm water, rinse, and let dry. If the original finish is intact, go straight to the priming stage.	Priming is not necessary unless you are changing from an oil-based to a water-based paint or are covering repairs. If you do not know whether an old paint surface is water- or oil-based, rub a small area with nail polish remover. If the paint comes off it is latex; if the area becomes shiny, it's oil. There are also swabs sold for this purpose.
mdf (new or previously painted)	Dust and wipe clean with a barely damp rag and let dry.	Fill in any nicks and holes with wood filler.	Sanding is not necessary on a new surface. If you are working on previously painted MDF and the paint has cracked or there are drip marks, sand smooth.	Use a water-based primer on new MDF.
plywood	Dust and wipe clean with a barely damp rag. Allow piece to dry thoroughly.	Fill in any nicks and nail and screw holes with wood filler.	Sand any very rough spots first with heavy-grade sandpaper, then complete the piece with medium- or fine-grade paper. Always work in the direction of the grain. Remove dust with a damp rag, vacuum, tack cloth.	Seal any knotholes with shellac.
concrete floors	Sweep, then wipe clean. Do not try to paint over a basement or ground-level concrete floor where dampness is a problem; the water moving through the concrete will lift the paint.	Fill any holes with concrete filler.	Sand any repairs smooth.	Prime with acrylic or oil-based primer.

glossary

alkyd or oil paint

Commercial oil-based paint used for coverage on walls. Less popular now than water-based paints. Clean up with paint thinner or turpentine.

anaglypta

An embossed wallpaper that is designed to be painted. Available in full-length patterned strips for walls and ceilings, shorter patterned panels for dados, as well as border widths.

artist's acrylics and artist's oils

Thick paint in tubes made from pure pigment. Used to tint glazing liquid when "true" colors, such as the earth tones raw sienna, burnt umber, and yellow ocher, are required. Artist's acrylics are water-based and must be mixed only with other water-based products. Similarly, artist's oils must be mixed only with oil-based products.

artist's brushes

Specialized brushes in different sizes and shapes that are used for hand-painting.

base coat

The first coat of paint applied over a primer. If a paint finish is to go over the top of the base coat, the recommended sheen is satin or pearl finish.

ceiling paint

A chalky, flat paint designed for ceiling application only. Extremely porous, it is difficult to clean and should never be used on walls. It is less expensive than standard wall paint.

chalk line

Used as a fast method to mark out a linear pattern on a wall or floor, it consists of a small container filled with powdered chalk and a coiled length of string. When the string is pulled out of the container, it is covered in a layer of chalk. The chalk is transferred when the string is pulled tight across a wall or floor and then pinged in the center, leaving a mark the same length as the string.

colored glaze

The medium produced when paint or colorants are mixed with a glazing liquid to produce a translucent color. See GLAZING LIQUID.

con-tact paper

Used traditionally for backing books and lining drawers. Available plain, colored, patterned, metallic, and mirrored, it has a very sticky backing that will adhere to most surfaces.

cork flooring

This renewable resource is very durable and soft and warm underfoot. Raw cork can be stained and painted before sealing with varnish. Available in a variety of colors and patterns.

crackle medium (crackle glaze)

A solution that when applied between two coats of latex paint causes the top coat to crack. The first coat of paint will be the color of the cracks, and the top coat will be the overall color of the surface.

crackle varnish (craquelure)

Sold as a kit, two varnish solutions with opposing properties are applied following package directions. As the top layer dries it separates into fine lines. Then a dark artist's oil paint such as burnt umber is rubbed over the surface to highlight the fine lines and cracks.

craft paper

Brown paper available by the roll that has many uses. It's perfect for making large templates or protecting areas that are not being worked on. Newspaper is an alternative, but it is very thin and can leave print marks on the work surface.

cutting in

When painting large surfaces such as walls and ceilings, a cutting-in brush with a tapered tip is used to apply paint to the edges in order to get a clean line. The rest of the surface can be painted with a roller.

denim brush

A plastic and rubber brick-shaped tool. One side has thick, hard plastic bristles rather like Velcro. When the brush is pulled through a wet colored glaze, it leaves irregular fine lines that create the look of a fabric weave like linen, silk, or denim. The brush is pulled through horizontally and vertically to produce the weavelike finish.

dragging brush

A coarse, long-bristle brush usually made from horsehair. When the brush is pulled through a colored glaze, it leaves the impression of fine lines. There are many alternatives to this professional tool. As long as the bristles are over 3 inches long, a wallpaper brush, broom, or a thick nylon bristle paintbrush can be used for dragging.

dry-brush painting

Certain paint effects, such as aging and stenciling, require the application of very little paint. Dip the brush into the paint and then remove the excess onto a paper towel or rag until the bristles are almost dry.

epoxol

A one-step, self-leveling top coat that goes on like a gel. This translucent durable coating is equivalent to fifty coats of regular varnish. See Faux Glass Floor, page 35.

finial

A decorative piece, generally made from wood or wrought iron, that attaches to the end of a curtain rod to stop the hooks or rings from falling off.

flogger

A long-hair bristle brush similar to a dragging brush. A flogged finish is produced by applying a colored glaze to a surface and then striking the wet glaze with the sides of the bristles.

frosted glass paint

A solution that when applied to glass will give the illusion of frosted glass. It is only semipermanent, as it will wash off if scrubbed.

gesso

A type of plaster used traditionally by artists to prepare a smooth surface on a canvas. The elastic in the gesso enables it to be used for other purposes, such as stenciling an image in relief, without the plaster cracking. You will find it at good paint stores and art supply stores. It can be pre-tinted or painted over when dry.

glazing liquid

A translucent colorless medium that when mixed with paint slows down the drying time of the paint. When added to paint, glazing liquid makes a colored glaze that allows you to create many paint effects. It will also make the paint translucent so that the base coat shows through the colored glaze. Both oil- and water-based glazing liquids are available and each must be added to the corresponding type of paint. You can color glazing liquid with standard oil or latex paint or artist's acrylics, oils, or colorants.

gloss paint

High-gloss paint is most often used on front doors, semigloss paint on baseboards, trim, and cabinets. The shinier surface makes it easy to clean, but it will show most imperfections.

jigsaw

An electrical handsaw designed for cutting intricate shapes into wood.

latex paint

Commercial water-based paint designed for good coverage over a large surface. Because latex dries fast, has only a slight, mild odor, and cleans up easily with soap and water, it is used more often than alkyd or oil paint. Available by the quart or gallon.

leaching

Stains such as nicotine, the resin from wood knots, ink, and water damage will show through a fresh coat of paint. These stains can be blocked with the proper surface primer.

level

A tool used to mark straight lines on a surface. A glass tube affixed to a metal ruler is partly filled with spirit and a bubble. When the bubble is centered you have a level line. It works on horizontal and vertical planes, and some levels even work on the diagonal.

low-tack painter's tape

A type of tape that is less sticky than traditional masking tape. When removed, it does not damage the surface by pulling off the existing base coat. It is used to seal off areas that do not require painting and for producing straight lines with paint. It is available in many different widths, from $\frac{1}{4}$ inch to 5 inches. There is even a bendable low-tack tape designed for taping around curves.

matte paint

Paint with a flat finish.

medium-density fiberboard (mdf)

A smooth and strong wood product made from wood fibers compressed tightly together. Available at lumber stores in various thicknesses, it is now the most common material used in the manufacture of furniture. Because it is so easy to cut with a jigsaw into shapes, it has many purposes in the home. New MDF must be primed before painting, and because there is no grain it is not ideal for staining.

metallic foil

Designed to be transferred onto a flat surface. Size is first applied to the surface and left to get tacky. The foil is then laid onto the surface with the metallic side facing out and burnished with a blunt object. When the top foil is peeled away, a metal veneer is left behind. Available by the roll in different metallic colors.

metallic paint

Commercial paints, usually water-based, available in a variety of metallic finishes, from different shades of gold, bronze, silver, and copper to metallics with a touch of color. Two coats are always required for an opaque finish.

opaque

The opposite of translucent; a coat of paint that hides the surface it covers. For maximum opacity, two coats are recommended.

open time

The time that paint, glaze, or varnish is wet and therefore able to be manipulated. Glazing liquid increases the open time and is mixed with paint so that you have time to create a pattern.

paint pens

Indelible pens used for painting straight lines on surfaces. They will not smudge when varnished.

pigment

Pure pigment, or color, comes in tubes as artist's acrylic or oil paint, or in powder form. A small amount is mixed with glazing liquid or regular latex or oil paint to produce the colors. When mixing powders, always wear a face mask.

plexiglas

A substitute for glass made from hard plastic, once again fashionable for use in furniture and accessories. It's sold by the sheet and can be cut into any size.

plumb line

A weight attached to a string. Although sold in hardware stores, you can make your own by tying a bobbin or metal spoon to a length of string. The top of the string is attached to the top of the wall with a pushpin or low-tack tape. Gravity will ensure that the string hangs perfectly straight. You can mark along the string with pencil on the wall and join up the marks when the plumb line is removed. Using a plumb line is a good way to mark out stripes on a vertical surface.

recipe

The proportions of paint, glazing liquid, and water that are mixed to produce the colored glazes used to create paint effects.

rocker or wood grainer

A tool designed for creating a faux wood finish. A piece of curved rubber that has grooves etched into the surface is attached to a handle. Pull the tool straight through a wet colored glaze while making a rocking motion with your wrist. The impression of the grain and knots seen in real wood planks is created.

rollers

There are several types of rollers, and each has its own purpose. All have a central hollow tube that slots onto a handle. Plastic inner tubes will last longer than cardboard. Long-pile rollers are used with paint or plaster for a textured finish. Short-pile rollers are used for smooth coverage of paint. Foam rollers can be used for applying a colored glaze before texturing or colorwashing with a rag or for applying varnish to large areas.

sandpaper

An abrasive paper used to make a surface smooth. Different grades of coarseness are available depending on the job at hand.

satin latex paint

A medium-luster paint, ideal as the base coat for most paint effects.

sea sponge

A natural sponge used for sponge painting. Although this paint effect is rather outdated today, sea sponges are a useful tool for other finishes like faux marble. They must be dampened before use and thoroughly washed out with soap and water.

silica sand

Found in craft stores, silica sand can be mixed into paint to add a fine texture. When this mixture is applied to a surface, the finish looks like suede.

size

A specialized glue used to adhere metallic leaf and foils to a surface.

spackle

Also known as caulking, a premixed plaster-based product used to fill nail holes and minor cracks in walls.

spray adhesive

An adhesive in a spray can often used for stenciling. It secures plastic or cardboard stencils flush to the surface while you work and pulls away easily for repositioning the stencil.

stencil

A shape, motif, or pattern cut out of Mylar, a strong thin plastic, waxed or unwaxed cardboard, or metal. A stencil can also be made from paper or self-stick paper such as MacTac, but neither material is reusable. Stencils are used to decorate a surface. The inside of the shape is covered with a very thin layer of paint and when the stencil is removed the image is on the surface. Plaster or gesso can also be applied over a stencil for an image in relief. Stenciling can be applied to most surfaces, including walls, furniture, fabrics, lampshades, and floors.

stencil brush

A flat-ended brush used for stippling or swirling the paint onto a stencil. Available in a variety of sizes. Always use one brush for each color, and use a dry brush to apply the paint in very thin coats. You can use other tools to fill in stencils: sponges, foam brushes, and rollers.

stippling tool

A professional stippling tool is brick-shaped with flat-ended bristles. The brush is pounced over a layer of wet colored glaze, giving the effect of tiny dots. Any flat-ended bristle brush can be used.

top coat

The last coat of paint, glaze, or varnish that is applied to the surface. It determines the sheen of your finished work.

translucent

Partially transparent. Refers to a coat of paint that has been mixed with glazing liquid, allowing the base coat to shine through.

upholstery studs

Metal studs used for upholstery. Available individually or in large rolls of attached studs where every tenth one requires nailing into the surface.

varnish

A translucent medium used to protect and add sheen to a surface, varnish is known by several names: polyurethane, urethane, clear coat, top coat. Available in flat, low-luster, semigloss, and high gloss, it is either oil-based or water-based. The latter has a milky look when in the can but dries clear. It's odorless and dries quickly. Most oil-based varnishes have a yellow tinge in the can and do yellow a surface in a relatively short time. There are non-yellowing varnishes available. Oil varnish must be applied over oil paint and can also be applied over water-based paint. Water-based varnish can be applied over latex paint but never over oil paint. Varnish can be tinted with a little paint or pigment. For smooth application, use varnish brush, a foam brush, or a foam roller.

varnish brush

A professional varnish brush is flat-ended with long bristles. Foam brushes work just as well; they are inexpensive, disposable, and will not leave lines in the varnish. Foam rollers should be used for large areas like floors.

venetian plaster

Plaster with marble dust added to it. When dry, the surface can be either left flat or polished with a metal spatula to a glasslike sheen. Venetian plaster is colored in the store by adding tints and then mixing thoroughly with an electric mixer. You can color it yourself by adding paint or pigment and stirring vigorously. When dry, the color is 40% lighter than when wet.

wallpaper paste

A thick glue for adhering wallpaper and Anaglypta to a wall.

x-acto knife

A sharp, adjustable blade used for many craft and home projects.

resources

If you have any difficulty finding the products and materials in this book, please access the Painted House website, where many products can be purchased or resourced in your area. The address is www.paintedhouse.com. or e-mail me at debbie@painted-house.com.

hot white living room

Epoxal 100 W.H. Clear
Ritins Studio Inc.
170 Wicksteed Avenue
Toronto, Ontario
M4G 2B6 Canada
Tel: (416) 467-8920
Fax: (416) 467-8963
www.ritins.com
info@ritins.com

Ritins Studio Inc. USA
c/o Modern Masters Inc.
7340 Greenbush Avenue
North Hollywood, CA
91605 USA
Tel: (800) 942-3166
Tel: (818) 765-2915
Fax: (818) 765-0013

fornasetti dining room

Fornasetti
Immaginazione S.r.l. Italy
www.fornasetti.com
fornasetti@planet.it

Dry Adhesive
Available at graphic arts stores or from
Graftek
P.O. Box 23260
Knoxville, TN
37933-1260 USA
Tel: (423) 777-9480
Fax: (423) 777-9482

Silver and Aluminum Leaf

Graftek
See above

Montreal Decorators
251 Ste. Catherine East
Montreal, Quebec
H2X IL5 Canada
Tel: (800) 215-6910

Fornasetti Lighting
Eurolite
5 Lower Sherbourne, Suite 100
Toronto, Ontario
M5A 2P3 Canada
Tel: (416) 203-1501

Green Painter's Tape
Tape Specialties
615 Bowes Road
Concord, Ontario
M5A 2P3 Canada
Tel: (905) 669-4881
Fax: (905) 669-2330

suburban update living room/ dining room

Frosted Glass Paint Kit
Available from **Delta** at most good craft stores, or at www.deltacrafts.com

Colored Metallic Leaf
Graftek
See above

now and zen living room

Artist's Molding Paste
Available at most good fine art stores, such as
Montreal Decorators
See above

Ornamental Gesso
Ritins Studio Inc.
See above

english living room

Damask Wallpaper Stencil
Dressler Stencil Company
253 SW 41st Street
Renton, WA 98055 USA
Tel: (888) 656-4515
Fax: (425) 656-4381
www.dresslerstencils.com

hemingway den

Bronze Metallic Transfer
Ritins Studio Inc.
See above

Aquasize
Available at good specialty art
supply stores, including
Montreal Decorators
See above

Ritins Studio, Inc.
See above

south seas loft

Fabric Dye and Color Remover
Available at drugstores and
craft stores

tuscany living room

Venetian Plaster
Martin & Associates
139 Labrosse
Pointe Claire, Quebec
H9R 1A3 Canada
Tel: (514) 697-3000
Fax: (514) 697-4116

Ritins Studio Inc.
See above

gothic revival dining room

Plastic Ceiling Tile
Ontario Wallcoverings/
Revêtements Muraux Concord
731 Millway Avenue
Concord, Ontario
L4K 3S8 Canada
Tel: (800) 563-2094
Fax: (905) 669-8920

arts and crafts dining room

Anaglypta Border
Steptoe & Wife Antiques
90 Tycos Drive
Toronto, Ontario
M6B 1V9 Canada
Tel: (800) 461-0060
www.steptoewife.com

index